Healthy Kitchen™

Batch cooking

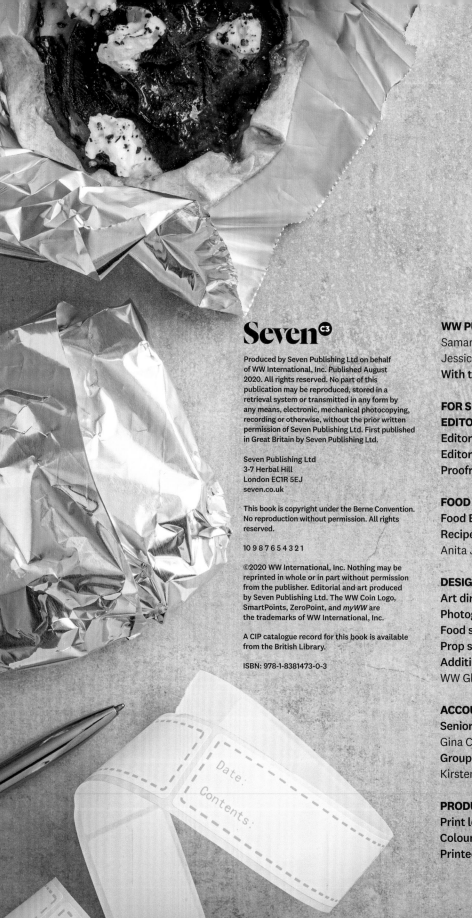

Seven C3

Produced by Seven Publishing Ltd on behalf of WW International, Inc. Published August 2020. All rights reserved. No part of this publication may be reproduced, stored in a retrieval system or transmitted in any form by any means, electronic, mechanical photocopying, recording or otherwise, without the prior written permission of Seven Publishing Ltd. First published in Great Britain by Seven Publishing Ltd.

Seven Publishing Ltd
3-7 Herbal Hill
London EC1R 5EJ
seven.co.uk

10 9 8 7 6 5 4 3 2 1

A CIP catalogue record for this book is available from the British Library.

ISBN: 978-1-8381473-0-3

WW PUBLICATIONS TEAM
Samantha Rees, Harriet Joy, Jessica O'Shea, Nicola Kirk.
With thanks to: Shelley Fletcher

FOR SEVEN PUBLISHING LTD
EDITORIAL
Editor-in-Chief: Helen Renshaw
Editor: Christine Faughlin
Proofreader: Sasha Turnbull

FOOD
Food Editor: Sarah Akhurst
Recipes: Sarah Akhurst, Anita Janusic, Abigail Spooner

DESIGN & PHOTOGRAPHY
Art director: Liz Baird
Photography: Ant Duncan
Food styling: Jenna Leiter
Prop styling: Davina Perkins
Additional photography: WW Global Asset Bank

ACCOUNT MANAGEMENT
Senior account manager: Gina Cavaciuti
Group publishing director: Kirsten Price

PRODUCTION
Print lead: Liz Knipe
Colour reproduction by F1 Colour
Printed in the UK by CPI Colour

Contents

6   Introduction

8   About our recipes

10   Batch-cook basics

14   Cook once, eat twice

42   3 ways with...

72   Batch bakes & frozen desserts

98   Cook the week

126   Indexes

Get ahead

We all want to eat well, but it can be hard to find the time to cook from scratch every day. The solution? Batch cooking! Whether you prefer a double-up approach of making one dish for now and another for the freezer, or would rather spend time at the weekend prepping meals for the week ahead, the aim is the same: to save you time and money. In this book, there are dishes to make now and enjoy later, meal plans to see you through a busy working week, goodies to stash in the freezer, and much more. With these simple and tasty recipes you'll have homecooked meals at the ready before you know it.

About our recipes

Our cookbooks are packed with recipes that are both nutritious and delicious...

Our philosophy is simple: to offer recipes that are nutritious as well as delicious. Our recipes are designed to encourage a healthier pattern of eating with lots of ZeroPoint™ foods and lower SmartPoints® value ingredients to make the most of your Budget. Here's how to better understand our recipes and the ingredients that go into them:

Ingredients

EGGS We use medium eggs, unless otherwise stated. Pregnant women, the elderly and children should avoid recipes with eggs which are raw or not fully cooked if not produced under the British Lion code of practice.

FRUIT AND VEGETABLES Recipes use medium-size fruit and veg, unless otherwise stated.

LOW-FAT SPREAD When a recipe uses a low-fat spread, we mean a spread with a fat content of no more than 39 per cent.

REDUCED-FAT SOFT CHEESE Where a recipe uses medium-fat soft cheese, we mean a soft cheese with 30 per cent less fat than its full-fat equivalent; where a recipe uses low-fat soft cheese, we mean a soft cheese with 5 per cent fat.

Prep and cook instructions

PREP AND COOK TIMES These are approximate and meant to be guidelines only. Prep time includes all steps up to and following the main cooking time(s). Stated cook times may vary according to your oven.

MICROWAVES If we've used a microwave in a recipe, the timings are for an 850-watt microwave oven.

Dietary requirements

VEGETARIAN RECIPES Recipes displaying a vegetarian symbol include non-meat ingredients, but may also contain processed products that aren't always vegetarian, such as pesto. If you're a vegetarian, ensure you use vegetarian varieties and check the ingredients labels. Where we reference vegetarian Italian-style hard cheese in vegetarian recipes, we mean a cheese similar to Parmesan (which is not vegetarian) but is suitable for vegetarians. For more information and guidance on vegetarianism, visit www.vegsoc.org

VEGAN RECIPES Recipes displaying a vegan symbol include no products made from or with the aid of animals or animal products. If you are vegan, you should ensure you use vegan varieties of processed ingredients (such as pesto) and check product labels to ensure ingredients have never been tested on animals. For more information and guidance on veganism, visit www.vegansociety.com

GLUTEN-FREE RECIPES Recipes that are labelled as gluten free include ingredients that naturally do not contain gluten, but they may also contain processed products, such as sauces, stock cubes and spice mixes. If so, you should ensure that those products do not include any gluten-containing ingredients (wheat, barley or rye) – these will be highlighted in the ingredients list on the product label. Manufacturers may also indicate whether there is a chance their product may have been contaminated with gluten during the manufacturing process. For more information and guidance on gluten-free products, visit www.coeliac.org.uk

NUT-FREE RECIPES Recipes displaying a nut free symbol include ingredients that do not contain nuts and/or certain seeds, but may include ingredients produced in facilities that also handle nut products. If you have a nut allergy, check ingredients labels for more information.

DAIRY-FREE RECIPES Recipes displaying a dairy free symbol include ingredients that naturally do not contain dairy, but may include ingredients produced in facilities that also handle dairy products. If you have a dairy allergy, check ingredients labels for more information.

SmartPoints calculations

SmartPoints values for the recipes in this book are calculated using the values for generic foods, not brands (except where stated). Tracking using branded items may affect the recorded SmartPoints. In line with the batch-cooking theme, many of the recipes in this book yield double or more quantities of a completed dish or components of a dish. The SmartPoints have been calculated per portion. If you reduce the quantities of the recipes in order to yield less, you'll need to recalculate for the most accurate SmartPoints.

WHEN YOU SEE THESE SYMBOLS:

Tells you the SmartPoints value per serving for each plan

Note: Recipes conform to the icon designations, but tip and serving suggestions may not.

 Indicates a recipe is gluten free

Indicates a recipe is vegetarian

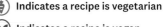 Indicates a recipe is vegan

 Indicates a recipe is nut free

  Indicates a recipe is dairy free

Batch-cook basics

Cooking healthy, nutritious meals in batches is as much about how you prep, cook and store your food as it is what you cook. Make it work every time with these helpful tips.

When it comes down to it, batch cooking is mostly about helping you to reclaim precious time. Once you get the hang of it, you'll undoubtedly find yourself spending far less time in the kitchen than usual. There'll be no more slaving at the hob when you get in from work, or standing aimlessly before an open fridge wondering how to magic up a meal from a random array of ingredients. But while you'll reduce the amount of hours you spend in the kitchen, you'll also become better acquainted with your fridge, freezer and the cupboard in which you store airtight containers – as our top tips for batch-cooking success show. We've covered everything from cooling, chilling and freezing, to defrosting, reheating and eating. Get to grips with those and you'll soon be batch cooking like a pro.

1 Check your kitchen kit

You don't need special equipment or fancy gadgets for batch-cooking success, although it is helpful to have some large pans and flameproof casserole dishes, for when you're cooking double batches. It also helps to have a few larger mixing bowls for prepping and a selection of ovenproof dishes for when you're making more than one complete meal, such as a pair of shepherd's pies.

2 Clear your containers

Do a stocktake of all your storage containers, ditching any that are cracked or leaking, and weeding out those with missing lids or seals. Invest in some additional plastic or glass containers that are both airtight and freezer-safe. It's a good idea to have a selection of sizes so you have the option to freeze in portions or larger batches – we love the Sistema 6 Pack to Go (£9.95, weightwatchersshop.co.uk). Sealable freezer bags are also worth stocking up on, especially if you have a smaller freezer. They're great space savers as you can freeze everything flat and fit more in your freezer. They also prevent freezer burn as, unlike containers, you can remove excess air out of the bag before sealing.

3 Stock up on kitchen foil, clingfilm and food wraps

Foil and clingfilm are essential for freezing whole, complete dishes, such

soup'n'sauce

CONTENTS: Mushroom Soup
DATE:
QUANTITY:

as pasta bakes or cakes. You'll need to tightly wrap the dish in clingfilm, followed by kitchen foil to prevent freezer burn. They also come in handy when storing goods in the fridge, as they keep odours in – and out. Consider also using reusable food wraps, such as beeswax wraps, for covering bowls and ingredients that you'll store in the fridge or at room temperature.

4 Cool and chill correctly

When you're prepping and cooking ahead of time, knowing how to cool and chill food safely is vital. First, check your fridge is at the correct temperature for chilling perishable foods – between 1°C and 7°C. When you have partially or completely cooked food that you want to store in the fridge or freezer, you must let it cool completely before wrapping and sealing. Once the food is completely cold, cover it with reusable lids, clingfilm or foil, before putting it into the fridge or freezer.

5 Know when to portion and when to pack whole

When packaging cooled food for the freezer or fridge, portion out soups, stews and curries into serving-size containers so you avoid defrosting the whole lot for just one person. For complete dishes, such as lasagne and pies, leave them in the original baking dish and freeze whole, so you can just defrost and reheat as it is. Each of the freezable recipes in this book has detailed instructions on how to store in the freezer, and for how long.

6 Label everything

If the aim of game is to save time, the last thing you want to do is spend time demystifying unidentifiable freezer goods. Use a permanent marker to clearly label each dish with its name, the date you froze it, how

'Clearly labelling each dish will help you to identify meals at a glance'

many portions it serves and the SmartPoints per serving. This will help you to identify meals at a glance. Store newer dishes towards the back of the freezer so you eat the older ones first.

7 Thaw and reheat safely

Always defrost frozen meals in the fridge overnight before cooking or reheating. Each of the recipes in this book gives clear instructions on whether the dish can be cooked or reheated from frozen or not. Many baked goods, such as breads and cakes, can be defrosted at room temperature – check the instructions accompanying each of the recipes. When a dish is cold, it takes longer than usual to reheat so let the chilled or defrosted dish come to room temperature before reheating.

Cook once, eat twice

16 **Beef & black bean stew**

18 **Sweet potato & goat's cheese rösti**

20 **Goan fish curry**

22 **Aubergine parmigiana bake**

24 **Braised cod with tomatoes, capers & olives**

26 **Pork & leek pie**

28 **Chicken paprikash**

30 **Chicken & chestnut mushroom lasagne**

32 **Chicken chipolata & prawn jambalaya**

34 **Lamb shepherd's pie**

36 **Cod & butter bean fishcakes**

38 **Chickpea tikka masala**

40 **Scotch broth**

Chipotle butternut squash soup

White bean & saffron soup

'Creamy' mushroom soup

Beef & black bean stew

serves 8   prep time 25 minutes   cook time 3 hours 10 minutes

   per serving

A hearty one-pot dish that provides plenty of warmth on a chilly evening. Rich and full of warming spices, it's perfect for ladling into big bowls and topping with fresh herbs.

Calorie controlled cooking spray

1.2kg beef braising steak, cut into 3cm pieces

2 red onions, diced

2 red peppers, deseeded and diced

3 garlic cloves, crushed

3 teaspoons ground cumin

3 teaspoons ground coriander

3-4 teaspoons mild chilli powder

1 cinnamon stick

6 large vine tomatoes, chopped

500ml beef stock, made with ½ stock cube

2 x 400g tins black beans, drained and rinsed

4 tablespoons roughly chopped fresh coriander

3 tablespoons roughly chopped fresh flat-leaf parsley

3 tablespoons roughly chopped fresh mint

1   Mist a large flameproof casserole with cooking spray and set over a medium-high heat. Cook the beef, in batches, for 8-10 minutes until browned all over. Use a slotted spoon to transfer the meat to a bowl.

2   Mist the casserole with more cooking spray and cook the onions and peppers, stirring, for 6-8 minutes or until softened. Add the garlic, spices and cinnamon stick and cook, stirring, for 1 minute.

3   Return the beef to the pan with the tomatoes and stock. Bring to the boil and then reduce the heat to low and simmer, covered, for 2 hours. Remove the lid and simmer for a further 30 minutes or until the beef is tender.

4   Add the black beans and simmer, uncovered, for 5 minutes or until the beans are heated through and the sauce has thickened. Remove and discard the cinnamon stick and stir through the herbs.

Cook's tip

This is a great stew to serve when you have friends over. Freeze both batches of the stew so that all you have to do on the day is reheat, then garnish and serve.

To serve

Divide half of the stew between 4 bowls, scatter over some extra coriander leaves and serve with lime wedges on the side.

To freeze

Store the remaining stew in an airtight container and freeze for up to 3 months. Defrost in the fridge overnight and reheat over a low heat on the hob, until piping hot throughout.

Sweet potato & goat's cheese rösti

makes 16   prep time 20 minutes   cook time 30 minutes

   per rösti

Great to have to hand in the freezer for brunches, lunches and light suppers, these versatile röstis combine the sweetness of sweet potato with the tang of goat's cheese.

1kg sweet potatoes, coarsely grated

Calorie controlled cooking spray

1 large red onion, finely diced

2 garlic cloves, crushed

250g hard goat's cheese, crumbled

4 tablespoons chopped fresh coriander

40g plain flour

2 eggs, beaten

1   Preheat the oven to 200°C, fan 180°C, gas mark 6. Put the grated sweet potato in a large bowl and set aside.

2   Mist a large nonstick frying pan with cooking spray and set over a medium heat. Fry the onion and garlic for 3-4 minutes until starting to soften.

3   Add the onion mixture to the bowl of sweet potato, followed by the goat's cheese, coriander, flour and eggs. Mix to combine, then season well and form the mixture into 16 röstis, squeezing to shape.

Cook's tip
You can freeze any leftover hard goat's cheese for up to 3 months. Just defrost and use another time.

To serve
For 4 people, mist a nonstick baking tray with calorie controlled cooking spray and add 8 of the rösti. Mist with cooking spray and bake for 20-25 minutes, until golden brown. Serve 2 röstis per person with a watercress and fresh tomato salad. The SmartPoints remain the same.

To freeze
Layer the remaining 8 röstis between pieces of baking paper and store in an airtight container in the freezer for up to 3 months. Defrost the röstis and cook and serve as per 'to serve' instructions.

Goan fish curry

serves 8   prep time 10 minutes   cook time 45 minutes

  per serving

This coconut-rich, hot and sour seafood curry is super easy to make
and is packed with delicious, quick-cook cod and prawns.

1 tablespoon cumin seeds

1½ tablespoons coriander seeds

Calorie controlled cooking spray

2 onions, finely sliced

4 garlic cloves, crushed

1 tablespoon grated ginger

1 teaspoon chilli flakes

1 teaspoon ground turmeric

20g light brown soft sugar

450g tomatoes, roughly chopped

2 star anise

2 x 400g tins reduced-fat coconut milk

600g skinless cod fillets, cut into large chunks

350g large peeled king prawns, deveined

1 Toast the cumin and coriander seeds for 1-2 minutes in a dry frying pan over a medium heat, until fragrant. Transfer to a pestle and mortar, then grind.

2 Mist a very large, deep frying pan with cooking spray and fry the onions for 6-8 minutes, or until soft and starting to caramelise. Add the garlic, ginger, chilli and turmeric and cook for 2 minutes.

3 Add the sugar and tomatoes and cook for 2-3 minutes, until the tomatoes are starting to soften. Add the star anise and coconut milk and bring to the boil. Reduce the heat and simmer for 15-20 minutes until the liquid has started to reduce. Add the cod and cook for 3 minutes, then add the prawns and cook for another 3 minutes. Season to taste and remove from the heat.

Cook's tip
You can use any firm white fish you like – just remember to adjust the SmartPoints for Green.

To serve
Cook 240g brown basmati rice (dry weight) to pack instructions, then divide between 4 bowls. Stir 100g young leaf spinach into half of the curry, then divide this between the bowls. Serve garnished with fresh coriander leaves.

To freeze
Store the remaining curry in an airtight container and freeze for up to 3 months. Defrost in the fridge overnight and reheat over a low heat on the hob, until piping hot throughout. Stir through the spinach to wilt, then serve as per 'to serve' instructions.

Aubergine parmigiana bake

serves 8 (makes 2 bakes)   **prep time 20 minutes**   **cook time 1 hour 25 minutes**

  1 per serving

Love lasagne, but don't always have the SmartPoints to spare?
Try this classic Italian vegetarian dish instead.

4 large aubergines, cut into 1cm-thick rounds

Calorie controlled cooking spray

2 onions, finely diced

3 garlic cloves, crushed

1 tablespoon dried oregano

3 x 400g tins chopped tomatoes

4 tablespoons chopped fresh basil

25g fresh white breadcrumbs

40g vegetarian Italian hard-style cheese, finely grated

1   Preheat the grill to high. Arrange one-third of the aubergine slices on a large baking sheet and mist all over with cooking spray. Cook under the grill for 3-5 minutes, then turn the aubergine, mist with more cooking spray and grill for another 3-5 minutes until tender and golden. Repeat with the remaining aubergine slices.

2   Mist a large nonstick pan with cooking spray and fry the onion with 2 tablespoons of water for 8-10 minutes, covered, over a medium heat until softened. Add the garlic and oregano and cook for 1 minute. Tip in the tinned tomatoes, stir and then let bubble, uncovered, for 15-20 minutes until thickened. Add the basil and season to taste.

3   Divide one-third of the tomato sauce between 2 baking dishes and top with half the aubergine slices. Top with another third of the sauce, followed by the remaining aubergine, and the remaining sauce. Combine the breadcrumbs and cheese, then scatter evenly over the top of each dish.

Cook's tip
Switch things up by using an equal mix of aubergine and courgette slices – you can prep and cook them the same way and the SmartPoints will remain the same.

To serve
Preheat the oven to 220°C, fan 200°C, gas mark 7. Bake one parmigiana for 25 minutes, until golden and bubbling. Scatter over a handful of fresh basil leaves and serve with a green salad on the side.

To freeze
Let the second parmigiana cool completely then cover with clingfilm followed by kitchen foil. Freeze for up to 3 months. Defrost overnight and then bake, uncovered, as per 'to serve' instructions.

Braised cod with tomatoes, capers & olives

serves 8   prep time 20 minutes   cook time 40 minutes

   per serving

A tasty fish and pasta one-pot meal that's sure to impress. Tender cod fillets are cooked gently on top of a rich and zesty orzo stew that's full of Mediterranean flavours.

8 x 120g fresh skinless cod fillets

Grated zest of 2 lemons, plus wedges to serve

Calorie controlled cooking spray

2 onions, finely chopped

3 celery sticks, finely chopped

3 garlic cloves, crushed

1½ tablespoons fennel seeds, lightly crushed

340g orzo

2 x 400g tins chopped tomatoes

900ml vegetable stock, made with 2 stock cubes

2 tablespoons capers, drained

70g pitted Kalamata olives, halved

1 Season the fish, then scatter over the lemon zest and set aside.

2 Mist a large deep, nonstick frying pan with cooking spray and fry the onions and celery over a medium-high heat for 6-8 minutes, covered, until softened. Add the garlic, fennel seeds and orzo and cook, stirring, for a further 2 minutes.

3 Stir in the tomatoes and stock and bring to the boil. Reduce the heat to low and simmer, covered, for 15 minutes, stirring occasionally. Add the capers and olives, and simmer, uncovered, for 5 minutes.

4 Transfer half the orzo mixture to a second frying pan set over a low heat. Add 4 cod fillets to each pan, spooning over some of the tomato mixture. Cover and simmer for 6-8 minutes until the fish is just opaque in the centre and the orzo is tender.

Cook's tip
You can use any firm white fish fillets you like – just remember to adjust the SmartPoints for Green.

To serve
Divide one pan of orzo and cod between 4 bowls and serve with lemon wedges on the side.

To freeze
Let the second pan of orzo and cod cool completely, then transfer to 1 large or 4 small airtight containers. Freeze for up to 3 months, then defrost in the fridge overnight. To reheat, decant into a large pan, cover and heat over a low heat on the hob, adding a splash of water to the orzo to loosen, until piping hot throughout.

Pork & leek pie

serves 8 (makes 2 pies)   **prep time 10 minutes**   **cook time 1 hour 5 minutes**

 per serving

A crisp, golden filo-topped pie is always a crowd-pleaser, and this tasty pork, leek and mustard version is no exception.

Calorie controlled cooking spray

1kg pork loin, cut into large cubes

1 onion, finely sliced

1kg leeks, trimmed and thinly sliced

2 garlic cloves, finely sliced

14 sage leaves, roughly chopped

20g plain flour

200ml chicken stock, made with ½ stock cube

200g 0% fat crème fraîche

2 tablespoons wholegrain mustard

6 x 45g sheets filo pastry

1   Mist a large nonstick pan with cooking spray and fry the pork, in batches, over a high heat for 2-3 minutes until browned all over. Transfer to a plate with a slotted spoon and set aside.

2   Reduce the heat to medium-low, mist the pan with cooking spray and fry the onions and leeks, covered, for 8-10 minutes, until soft. Add the garlic and sage and cook for 2 minutes, then add the flour and cook for another 2 minutes. Return the pork to the pan.

3   In a jug, combine the stock and crème fraîche, then add this mixture to the pan with the mustard. Bring the mixture to the boil, then reduce the heat and simmer for 2 minutes. Divide the filling between 2 large pie dishes (measuring 25cm x 17cm).

4   Preheat the oven to 200°C, fan 180°C, gas mark 6. Unroll one sheet of the pastry, keeping the others covered, and mist all over with cooking spray. Scrunch and place on top of one of the pies. Repeat so you have 3 sheets on each pie. Mist again with cooking spray then bake both pies for 30-35 minutes, until the pastry is golden brown.

Cook's tip
You can use any pastry topping you like for this pie – or even mashed root veg. Just remember to adjust the SmartPoints.

To serve
Steam 320g Tenderstem broccoli or fine green beans, and serve alongside one of the cooked pies.

To freeze
Allow the second pie to cool completely, then cover with clingfilm followed by kitchen foil and freeze for up to 3 months. To serve, preheat the oven to 200°C, fan 180°C, gas mark 6 and reheat the pie from frozen for 1 hour, until it's piping hot throughout.

Chicken paprikash

serves 8   **prep time 20 minutes**   **cook time 45 minutes**

  per serving

Inspired by the classic Hungarian stew, this creamy, paprika-infused chicken and mushroom dish is an easy family-friendly option.

Calorie controlled cooking spray

750g skinless chicken breast fillets, cut into strips

2 red onions, diced

2 green peppers, deseeded and sliced

3 tablespoons paprika

30g plain flour

800ml chicken stock, made with 2 stock cubes

450g chestnut mushrooms, sliced

200g reduced-fat soured cream

4 tablespoons chopped fresh dill

1   Mist a large flameproof casserole with cooking spray and set over a high heat. Season the chicken, then fry it in batches for 3 minutes on each side, until browned all over. Transfer the chicken to a plate and set aside.

2   Mist the casserole again, then fry the onions and peppers, covered, over a medium heat for 8-10 minutes, until softened and lightly browned. Add the paprika and flour and cook, stirring constantly, for 1 minute. Gradually add the stock and cook, stirring, until the mixture bubbles and thickens slightly. Stir in the mushrooms and simmer for 3 minutes. Return the chicken to the casserole, reduce the heat and simmer for 5 minutes, covered, until the chicken is cooked through.

3   Stir through the soured cream and dill. Bring to a gentle simmer, then remove from the heat.

Cook's tip
This dish is so versatile – you can also serve it alongside rice or mashed veg, or use it as a pie filling. Just remember to adjust the SmartPoints.

To serve
Cook 4 x 50g egg noodle nests (we used Blue Dragon) to pack instructions and divide between 4 bowls. Spoon over half the paprikash and top with extra dill.

To freeze
Store the remaining paprikash in an airtight container and freeze for up to 3 months. Defrost in the fridge overnight and reheat over a low heat on the hob, until piping hot throughout.

Chicken & chestnut mushroom lasagne

serves 8 (makes 2 lasagne)   **prep time 30 minutes**   **cook time 1 hour 45 minutes**

   per serving

A delicious twist on a classic lasagne made with layers of chicken, veg and cheese sauce.

Calorie controlled cooking spray

4 leeks, trimmed and thinly sliced

700g skinless chicken breast fillets, cut into 2-3cm cubes

3 tablespoons chopped fresh tarragon

450g chestnut mushrooms, sliced

3 garlic cloves, crushed

400g young leaf spinach

12 WW Yellow Lentil Lasagne Sheets

30g Parmesan, grated

FOR THE CHEESE SAUCE

800ml semi-skimmed milk

30g cornflour

250g medium-fat soft cheese

Grated zest of 1 lemon

1 Mist a nonstick pan with cooking spray. Add the leeks and 2 tablespoons water and cook, uncovered, for 10 minutes. Transfer to a bowl. Mist the pan again and fry the chicken, in batches, for 10 minutes until cooked. Add to the bowl of leeks, stir in the tarragon and season.

2 Mist the pan again, fry the mushrooms for 5 minutes, then add the garlic and spinach and cook, covered, for 3 minutes. Increase the heat and cook, uncovered, until the liquid evaporates. Season and set aside.

3 To make the cheese sauce, mix 3 tablespoons of the milk with the cornflour in a jug to form a paste, then stir in the remaining milk. Pour the mixture into a pan, add the soft cheese and cook over a low heat, stirring, until smooth. Bring to a boil and cook for 2 minutes, or until thickened. Season and stir through the lemon zest.

4 To assemble, divide one-third of the cheese sauce between 2 medium baking dishes (around 25cm x 17cm). Top each with one-quarter of the chicken mixture followed by 3 lasagne sheets. Divide the spinach mixture between the 2 dishes, then repeat with the cheese sauce, chicken mixture and lasagne sheets. Finish with a layer of cheese sauce, then scatter over the Parmesan.

To make
Use WW Yellow Lentil Lasagne Sheets instead of regular. They're made from yellow lentil and brown rice flour, are gluten free and high in protein. Available at the WW online shop.

To serve
Preheat the oven to 200°C, fan 180°C, gas mark 6 and bake one of the lasagnes for 40-45 minutes until golden and bubbling. Serve with a green salad.

To freeze
Cover the second uncooked lasagne with clingfilm and then kitchen foil, and freeze for up to 3 months. Defrost in the fridge overnight and bake, uncovered, as per 'to serve' instructions.

Chicken chipolata & prawn jambalaya

serves 8   prep time 20 minutes   cook time 50 minutes

7 **6** **6** per serving

This Cajun-inspired rice dish is the perfect bowl food for nights spent in front of the telly.

Calorie controlled cooking spray

340g pack Heck Simply Chicken Chipolatas

2 onions, finely diced

3 sweet pointed peppers, deseeded and roughly chopped

4 garlic cloves, crushed

2 teaspoons dried oregano

3 teaspoons smoked paprika

¼ teaspoon cayenne pepper

350g paella rice

1 litre chicken stock, made with 2 stock cubes

2 x 400g tins chopped tomatoes

3 sprigs thyme

450g raw peeled king prawns, deveined

200g frozen peas

4 tablespoons chopped fresh flat-leaf parsley

4 tablespoons lemon juice

1 Mist a large nonstick frying pan with cooking spray and cook the chipolatas over a medium-high heat for 8-10 minutes, turning occasionally. Set aside on a plate, then cut into thick slices on the diagonal.

2 Mist a large nonstick pan with cooking spray, add the onions, peppers and 2 tablespoons water and cook, covered, for 5 minutes over a medium heat. Stir, then cook, uncovered, for a further 5 minutes, until softened and just starting to colour.

3 Add the garlic, oregano and spices and cook, stirring, for 1-2 minutes. Stir in the rice so it is well coated, then pour in the stock, tomatoes and thyme. Season well, bring to a simmer and cook, covered, for 20 minutes, stirring once or twice. Stir the chipolatas through the jambalaya, along with the prawns and peas. Leave to cook, covered, for 5-7 minutes or until the rice, peas and prawns are cooked through, the chipolatas are piping hot and the liquid has been absorbed.

4 Remove and discard the thyme sprigs, then season to taste and stir through the parsley and lemon juice.

Cook's tip
You can use any chicken or turkey sausages in this recipe – just remember to adjust the SmartPoints.

To serve
Divide half of the jambalaya between 4 bowls, then scatter over a little extra chopped parsley. Serve with lemon wedges.

To freeze
Store the remaining jambalaya in an airtight container and freeze for up to 3 months. Defrost overnight in the fridge and reheat over a low heat on the hob, adding a splash of water, until hot throughout.

Lamb shepherd's pie

serves 8 (makes 2 pies)   **prep time 35 minutes**   **cook time 2 hours 15 minutes**

   per serving

When it comes to comforting family dinners, a classic shepherd's pie is hard to beat. We've topped ours with a kale, horseradish and butternut squash mash.

Calorie controlled cooking spray

1kg lean lamb mince (10% fat)

2 red onions, finely diced

2 carrots, finely diced

3 celery sticks, finely diced

3 garlic cloves, finely sliced

8 sprigs thyme, leaves stripped

30g plain flour

30g tomato purée

1 litre beef stock, made with 2 stock cubes

4 tablespoons Worcestershire sauce

1.2kg butternut squash (prepared weight), cut into large chunks

200g shredded kale

2 tablespoons horseradish sauce

1 Mist a large flameproof casserole with cooking spray and fry the mince, in batches, over a high heat for 8-10 minutes. Transfer to a bowl with a slotted spoon and set aside. Mist the casserole again, then cook the onions, carrots and celery, stirring occasionally, over a medium heat for 8-10 minutes, covered, until soft. Add the garlic and thyme and cook for 1 minute.

2 Add the flour and cook, stirring constantly, for 2 minutes. Return the lamb to the casserole with the tomato purée, stock and Worcestershire sauce and bring to the boil. Reduce the heat to low, cover, and simmer for 30 minutes. Remove the lid and cook for a further 30-40 minutes until the sauce has thickened.

3 Meanwhile cook the butternut squash in a large pan of boiling water for 20 minutes, until tender. Drain, then season and mash. While the squash is cooking, put the kale in a microwave-safe bowl, cover and microwave on High for 2 minutes until wilted. Stir the kale and horseradish sauce through the mash.

4 Divide the mince mixture between 2 medium baking dishes (about 25cm x 17cm) and spoon over the mash.

Cook's tip
Rather than 2 large pies, you can make 8 individual pies. The smaller pies will take approximately 20 minutes to cook.

To serve
Preheat the oven to 200°C, fan 180°C, gas mark 6 and bake one of the pies for 25 minutes, or until the filling is bubbling. Serve with 320g steamed green beans. The SmartPoints will remain the same.

To freeze
Cover the uncooked shepherd's pie with clingfilm and then kitchen foil, and freeze for up to 3 months. Defrost in the fridge overnight and bake, uncovered, as per 'to serve' instructions.

Cod & butter bean fishcakes

makes 16   prep time 20 minutes + chilling   cook time 15 minutes

   per fishcake

Fishcakes are a great freezer staple as they're handy for both lunch and dinner, and are ready portioned so you can just help yourself to as many as you need.

400g potatoes, cut into chunks

20g low-fat spread

1 lemon, ½ sliced and ½ zested

3 sprigs fresh flat-leaf parsley, plus 1 tablespoon finely chopped parsley

½ teaspoon black peppercorns

800g skinless cod fillets

80g cornichons

2 tablespoons chopped fresh chives

2 tablespoons Dijon mustard

400g tin butter beans, drained and rinsed

80g panko breadcrumbs

1 Cook the potatoes in a pan of boiling water for 12-15 minutes until tender. Drain, mash with the low-fat spread, then season and set aside.

2 Meanwhile, put 1 litre water in a pan with the lemon slices, parsley sprigs and peppercorns. Bring to a simmer then reduce the heat to low, add 400g of the cod and poach for 4-5 minutes. Lift from the water using a slotted spoon, then flake into large chunks and set aside. Discard the poaching water.

3 Put the remaining cod, cornichons, chives, mustard and butter beans into a food processor. Season and pulse until well combined. Scrape the mixture into a bowl, add the mashed potato and stir to combine. Season well and gently fold the flaked fish into the mixture. Shape into 16 patties.

4 Combine the zest, breadcrumbs and chopped parsley with some seasoning on a plate. Press both sides of each of the patties into the crumb to give a light coating, then chill in the fridge for 20 minutes before cooking.

Cook's tip
Make a tartare sauce to serve 4 people. Mix 200g Lighter than Light Mayonnaise (we used Hellmann's) with 2 tablespoons each chopped capers, gherkins and fresh flat-leaf parsley. Stir in 1 chopped shallot and the juice of ½ lemon. Season to taste.

To serve
Preheat the oven to 200°C, fan 180°C, gas mark 6. Heat ½ teaspoon of olive oil in a nonstick frying pan over a medium heat. Mist 8 of the fishcakes with cooking spray, then cook, in batches, for 4 minutes on each side. Transfer to a baking sheet, mist again and bake for 20 minutes until golden.

To freeze
Layer the uncooked fishcakes between pieces of baking paper then freeze in an airtight container for up to 3 months. Defrost in the fridge overnight, then cook as per 'to serve' instructions.

Chickpea tikka masala

serves 8   **prep time 10 minutes**   **cook time 35 minutes**

   per serving

A satisfying, budget-friendly curry that's oh-so easy to make and freeze.
If you like your curries to be really hot, simply add more chillies.

Calorie controlled cooking spray

2 onions, finely diced

4 garlic cloves, crushed

2 teaspoons finely chopped ginger

1 red chilli, deseeded and chopped

1½ tablespoons garam masala

2 teaspoons ground cumin

1 teaspoon paprika

1½ tablespoons tomato purée

3 x 400g tins chickpeas, drained
and rinsed

3 x 400g tins chopped tomatoes

400ml tin reduced-fat coconut milk

Juice of 1 lime

1 Mist a very large nonstick pan with cooking spray
   and cook the onion with 2 tablespoons of water
   and a pinch of salt, covered, for 8-10 minutes, until
   softened. Add the garlic, ginger, chilli and spices and
   cook, stirring, for a further 1-2 minutes, until fragrant.

2 Stir in the tomato purée, and cook, stirring, for
   1 minute. Tip in the chickpeas, tomatoes and coconut
   milk. Bring the mixture to the boil then reduce the
   heat and simmer for 20 minutes.

3 Stir in the lime juice and season to taste.

Cook's tip
Serve with 1 x 43g WW Mini
Garlic & Coriander Naan
Bread per person, warmed
to pack instructions.

To serve
Blitz 1 cauliflower in a food processor
until it's the texture of rice, then
transfer to a microwave-safe bowl.
Cover then microwave on High for 5-6
minutes. Divide between 4 bowls, top
with half of the tikka masala and serve
garnished with chopped fresh coriander.

To freeze
Allow the remaining tikka masala
to cool completely then freeze
in an airtight container for up to
3 months. Defrost and reheat
gently on the hob, until piping
hot throughout.

Batch-cook soups

Few dishes lend themselves better to batch cooking than soup – make a nourishing pot, then stash individual portions in the freezer ready to defrost for lunch or dinner.

Scotch broth

serves 8   prep time 35 mins   cook time 1 hr 20 mins

   per serving

Roughly chop 3 **turnips**, 3 **carrots**, 2 **leeks**, and 2 **onions**, then slice 500g **lean lamb leg steaks** into strips. Mist a large nonstick pan with **calorie controlled cooking spray** and brown the lamb, in batches, over a high heat for 5-6 minutes. Remove from the pan. Mist the pan again and add the prepped veg, 2 tablespoons chopped **fresh thyme**, 2 **bay leaves** and 3 **rosemary sprigs**. Cook, covered, for 10 minutes. Add 2 litres of **lamb or chicken stock** (made with 2 stock cubes) and 90g **pearl barley**. Bring to the boil, then reduce the heat, cover and simmer for 50 minutes. Return the lamb to the pot and cook for 10 minutes. Season, discard the bay leaf and rosemary, and stir in 6 tablespoons chopped **fresh flat-leaf parsley**.
TO SERVE Divide half the soup between bowls and serve garnished with extra chopped fresh flat-leaf parsley.
TO FREEZE Let the rest of the soup cool completely, then freeze in containers or pouches for up to 3 months. Defrost then reheat over a low heat on the hob until piping hot.

Chipotle butternut squash soup

serves 8   prep time 15 mins   cook time 40 mins

   per serving

Preheat the oven to 200°C, fan 180°C, gas mark 6. Put 1.5kg peeled and cubed **butternut squash** in 2 roasting tins and mist with **calorie controlled cooking spray**. Season then roast for 35-40 minutes. Meanwhile, mist a large nonstick pan with cooking spray and fry 2 sliced **onions** for 8-10 minutes, until soft. Add 2 teaspoons **dried oregano**, 2 sliced **garlic** cloves, 1 tablespoon **chipotle paste** and the grated zest of 1 **orange**, then cook for 2 minutes. Add the roasted squash to the pot and pour over 1.25 litres hot **chicken stock** (made with 2 stock cubes). Use a stick blender to purée, then season.
TO SERVE Dry fry 80g diced **chorizo** in a nonstick frying pan for 2-3 minutes. Divide half of the soup between 4 bowls and scatter over the chorizo.

TO FREEZE Let the remaining soup cool completely, then freeze in containers or pouches for up to 3 months. Defrost then reheat over a low heat on the hob until piping hot.

White bean & saffron soup

serves 8   prep time 15 mins   cook time 25 mins

   per serving

Finely dice 1 **onion**, 3 **celery** sticks and 1 **carrot** and set aside. Mist a large nonstick pan with **calorie controlled cooking spray** and fry the prepared veg, covered, for 8-10 minutes, until soft. Drain and rinse 2 x 400g tins **cannellini beans** and add to the pan with a pinch of **saffron** threads and 1 litre **vegetable stock** (made with 1 stock cube). Bring to the boil then reduce the heat and simmer for 10 minutes. Stir in 150g **half-fat crème fraîche**, then use a stick blender to purée. Season to taste.
TO SERVE Divide half the soup between 4 bowls and top with 1 diced **red chilli** and some **fresh coriander**.
TO FREEZE Let the remaining soup cool completely, then freeze in containers or pouches for up to 3 months. Defrost then reheat over a low heat on the hob until piping hot.

'Creamy' mushroom soup

serves 8   prep time 20 mins   cook time 20 mins

   per serving

Put 450g prepared **cauliflower rice** (we used Tesco) in a microwave-safe bowl. Cover and microwave on High for 5 minutes. Mist a very large nonstick frying pan with **calorie controlled cooking spray** and fry 2 finely diced **shallots** and 4 crushed **garlic** cloves for 3 minutes. Add 450g sliced **chestnut mushrooms**, 150g chopped **mixed mushrooms** and 2 tablespoons chopped **fresh thyme**. Cook, stirring occasionally, for 7-8 minutes, until any liquid has evaporated. Transfer one-quarter of the mushroom mixture to a blender, add the cooked cauliflower rice and 900ml **vegetable stock** (made with 1 stock cube) and blend until smooth. Return to the pan of mushrooms and season to taste.
TO SERVE Divide half the soup between 4 bowls and serve topped with extra thyme leaves.
TO FREEZE Let the remaining soup cool completely, then freeze for up to 3 months. Defrost then reheat over a low heat on the hob until piping hot.

3 ways with...

46 Lentil & cauliflower dhal
Dhal with mango chutney chicken

47 Roti-style wraps with dhal
Dhal traybake with
spiced salmon

50 Soy-poached chicken
breast fillets
Soy-poached chicken with
ginger fried rice

51 Chinese pancakes with
soy-poached chicken
Chinese soy-poached
chicken noodle soup

54 Rich Quorn ragù
Lentil spaghetti with Quorn ragù

55 Indian-spiced Quorn
ragù pot pies
Quorn ragù tortilla bake

58 Pork polpette
Sticky hoisin pork
polpette with rice

59 Sicilian pork polpette bake
Pork polpette pittas with
harissa yogurt

62 Quinoa-crusted fish goujons
Crispy fish tacos with lime
slaw & mango salsa

63 Fish goujons with
Mexican-style rice
Fish goujons with crushed
ricotta peas

66 Kale pesto
Fusilli with kale
pesto & tomatoes

67 Chicken, mushroom
& kale pesto pizza
Pesto chicken cobbler

70 Greek yogurt cake
Lemon meringue
pie cake

71 Strawberry syrup cake
Orange & pistachio cake

Three ways with...
Lentil & cauliflower dhal

Take one creamy, spicy dhal that's big on flavour and packed with good-for-you ingredients, and spin it into three completely different but equally satisfying suppers.

Master recipe
Lentil & cauliflower dhal

serves 12   **prep time 10 mins**   **cook time 1 hr 15 mins**

   per serving

A warming dish that's fragrant with spices. If you prefer it hot, simply toss in a few extra chillies.

1 large cauliflower, broken into florets
1 tablespoon rapeseed oil
1 tablespoon cumin seeds
Calorie controlled cooking spray
2 onions, finely sliced
3 garlic cloves, crushed
30g ginger, grated
1 green chilli, thinly sliced
1½ tablespoons ground turmeric
3 tablespoons garam masala
6 tomatoes, roughly chopped
750g red split lentils
1.8 litres vegetable stock, made with 2 stock pots

1   Preheat the oven to 200°C, fan 180°C, gas mark 6. Put the cauliflower in a roasting tin and drizzle over the oil. Season and roast for 30 minutes.
2   Meanwhile, toast the cumin seeds in a dry frying pan for 1-2 minutes until fragrant, then grind them using a pestle and mortar.
3   Mist a large flameproof casserole with cooking spray and fry the onions for 8-10 minutes, until softened. Add the garlic, ginger, chilli, spices and ground cumin seeds, then cook for 1-2 minutes. Add the tomatoes and cook for another 2 minutes.
4   Stir in the lentils and stock, then bring the mixture to the boil. Reduce to a simmer and cook, covered, for 1 hour, until the lentils are tender. Add a splash of water if the dhal starts to look dry.
5   Stir through the roast cauliflower and season to taste, then set aside to cool completely before portioning and freezing.

TO FREEZE Divide the cooled dhal equally between 3 airtight containers and freeze for up to 3 months. Defrost overnight at room temperature.

One
Dhal with mango chutney chicken

serves 4
prep time 5 mins + marinating   **cook time 10 mins**

   per serving

Sweet, sticky chicken on a bed of spinach dhal.

150g 0% fat natural Greek yogurt
2 tablespoons mango chutney
4 x 165g skinless chicken breast fillets, cut into strips
Calorie controlled cooking spray
1 x quantity lentil & cauliflower dhal, defrosted
100g young leaf spinach

1   In a large bowl, mix together the yogurt and chutney. Add the chicken and stir to coat. Cover and marinate in the fridge for 30 minutes.
2   Mist a large nonstick griddle pan with cooking spray and griddle the chicken for 8-10 minutes, turning occasionally, until cooked through. You may need to do this in batches.
3   Meanwhile, warm the dhal in a large pan over a medium heat until piping hot. Stir in the spinach, cover, and cook for 2 minutes, until the spinach has wilted.
4   Divide the spinach dhal between plates, top with the mango chicken and serve.

COOK'S TIP To make this recipe vegan, use 396g firm tofu in place of chicken and plain soya yogurt instead of dairy. The SmartPoints will remain the same.

Two
Roti-style wraps with dhal

serves 4
prep time 10 mins + resting   cook time 10 mins

   per serving

Homemade bread that's ready in next to no time.

1 x quantity lentil & cauliflower dhal, defrosted
80g young leaf spinach
3 tablespoons chopped fresh coriander, plus extra to serve
80g 0% fat natural Greek yogurt
¼ cucumber, grated

FOR THE ROTI-STYLE BREAD
150g self-raising flour, plus an extra 10g for dusting
1 tablespoon vegetable oil
½ teaspoon sea salt

1   To make the roti-style bread, sift the flour into a bowl then stir in the oil and salt. Slowly add 75ml warm water and mix until it comes together into a dough. Turn it out onto a floured surface and knead for 2-3 minutes. Cover and set aside for 10 minutes.

2   Divide the dough into 4 pieces, roll into balls then cover and set aside. Roll out one of the balls to a thin 20-22cm circle. Heat a dry frying pan over a high heat and cook the dough for 30-45 seconds on each side, until it bubbles and starts to brown in spots. Keep warm under a clean tea towel and repeat with the remaining dough.

3   Meanwhile, warm the dhal in a large pan over a medium heat until piping hot, then stir through the spinach and 2 tablespoons of the coriander.

4   In a bowl, combine the yogurt, cucumber and the remaining 1 tablespoon of coriander. Season.

5   To serve, spoon the dhal over one half of each roti, then top with the cucumber yogurt. Scatter over the extra coriander then fold and serve.

Three
Dhal traybake with spiced salmon

serves 4   prep time 5 mins   cook time 40 mins

   per serving

The ultimate Friday night supper – tender fish fillets baked with dhal and topped with herbs.

1 tablespoon rapeseed oil
2 red onions, finely sliced
1 x quantity lentil & cauliflower dhal, defrosted
4 x 130g skinless salmon fillets
1 tablespoon garam masala
Calorie controlled cooking spray
20g toasted flaked almonds, to serve
Handful of fresh coriander leaves, to serve

1   Preheat the oven to 200°C, fan 180°C, gas mark 6. Heat the oil in a nonstick frying pan over a medium heat and fry the onions, stirring continuously, for 8-10 minutes until they start to colour and crisp up. Remove from the heat and set aside.

2   Meanwhile, put the dhal in a roasting tin and bake in the oven for 15 minutes.

3   Toss the salmon in the garam masala. Mist a nonstick frying pan with cooking spray and fry the fish for 1 minute on each side, or until just coloured. Arrange the fish on top of the dhal and bake for a further 10-12 minutes until the salmon is cooked through and the dhal is piping hot throughout.

4   To serve, divide the lentils and salmon between plates and scatter over the crispy onions, toasted almonds and coriander.

Three ways with...
Soy-poached chicken

Tenderly poach a batch of skinless chicken breast fillets in an aromatic Chinese-style broth and you'll have the tasty foundations of three winning chicken dinners.

Master recipe
Soy-poached chicken breast fillets

makes 10 chicken breasts
prep time 10 mins   cook time 20 mins

   per serving

Poaching fillets in broth results in juicy, flavour-infused chicken that freezes well.

150ml soy sauce
3 tablespoons mirin
1 tablespoon light brown soft sugar
4 garlic cloves, sliced
4 spring onions, sliced
2 teaspoons grated ginger
1 teaspoon black peppercorns
1 tablespoon Chinese 5 spice
10 x 165g skinless chicken breast fillets

1 Put all of the ingredients, except the chicken, into your largest pan and bring the mixture to a gentle simmer. Lower the chicken breasts into the pan then top up with just enough water for the mixture to cover the chicken. Bring the mixture back to a simmer and cover the pan with a lid. Poach the chicken for 15 minutes, or until cooked through.

2 Lift the chicken from the poaching liquid, using a slotted spoon, and set aside to cool completely. Discard the poaching liquid, or strain it and let cool completely before freezing in airtight containers for use in soups and stews.

TO FREEZE Put the poached chicken fillets into individual freezer bags and freeze for up to 3 months. Defrost overnight in the fridge then bring to room temperature before eating or reheating.

One
Soy-poached chicken with ginger fried rice

serves 4   prep time 5 mins   cook time 20 mins

  per serving

Satisfying and quick to whip up, this is the perfect dish to make on busy weeknights.

250g basmati rice
4 pak choi, halved
1 tablespoon sesame oil
2 garlic cloves, finely sliced
20g ginger, cut into matchsticks
Handful of coriander, roughly chopped
2 tablespoons soy sauce
½ teaspoon chilli flakes
4 soy-poached chicken breast fillets, defrosted

1 Cook the rice to pack instructions, then drain and set aside to steam dry. Meanwhile, put the pak choi in a large, shallow pan and cover with boiling water from the kettle. Simmer for 2-3 minutes over a low heat until just tender, then drain and set aside.

2 Heat half the oil in a nonstick wok or frying pan and stir-fry the garlic and ginger for 2 minutes over a medium heat. Add the rice and stir-fry for 2-3 minutes, then season and stir though the coriander.

3 Meanwhile, heat the remaining oil in a large nonstick frying pan and add the steamed pak choi with the soy sauce and chilli. Stir-fry for 1-2 minutes.

4 Warm the chicken through in the microwave until piping hot throughout and cut into bite-size pieces. Serve with the ginger rice and pak choi.

COOK'S TIP To reduce the SmartPoints on Purple, use 250g brown Basmati rice instead of white and calorie controlled cooking spray instead of sesame oil.

Two
Chinese pancakes with soy-poached chicken

serves 4   prep time 10 mins   cook time 5 mins

   per serving

Love Chinese duck pancakes? This low SmartPoints chicken version is just as tasty.

30g hoisin sauce
1 tablespoon sweet chilli sauce
Calorie controlled cooking spray
2 soy-poached chicken breast fillets, defrosted and shredded
8 x 10g Chinese pancakes
1 small carrot, cut into matchsticks
⅓ cucumber, cut into matchsticks
3 spring onions, trimmed and shredded

1   In a small bowl, combine the hoisin sauce and sweet chilli sauce and set aside.
2   Mist a large nonstick frying pan with cooking spray and fry the shredded chicken for 2-3 minutes, or until warmed through. Toss the sauce though the chicken and keep warm.
3   Warm the pancakes in the microwave to pack instructions. To serve, fill each pancake with some of the shredded chicken, then top with the carrot, cucumber and spring onions.

Three
Chinese soy-poached chicken noodle soup

serves 4   prep time 15 mins   cook time 15 mins

   per serving

Ready in just half an hour, this hearty chicken noodle soup is brimming with fresh flavours.

Calorie controlled cooking spray
2 garlic cloves, finely sliced
15g ginger, cut into matchsticks
125g shiitake mushrooms, torn
1.5 litres chicken stock, made with 2 stock pots
2 tablespoons soy sauce
1 tablespoon hoisin sauce
1-2 teaspoons chilli sauce
200g dried egg noodles
4 soy-poached chicken breast fillets, defrosted and shredded
150g frozen edamame beans
2 carrots, peeled into ribbons
100g choi sum
1 red chilli, finely sliced
2 spring onions, trimmed and shredded lengthways
Handful of coriander leaves, to serve

1   Mist a large nonstick pan with cooking spray and fry the garlic and ginger for 2 minutes. Add the mushrooms and fry for 3-4 minutes.
2   Stir in the chicken stock, soy sauce, hoisin sauce and chilli sauce. Bring to the boil, then add the noodles, shredded chicken and edamame. Simmer for 6-7 minutes, adding the carrot and choi sum for the final 2 minutes, until the noodles are cooked and the chicken is piping hot.
3   Divide between bowls and serve garnished with the chilli, spring onions and coriander.

Three ways with...
Quorn ragù

With a large pot of rich Quorn ragù bubbling away on the
hob, you'll never be short of tasty veggie suppers.

Master recipe
Rich Quorn ragù

serves 12   **prep time 20 mins**   **cook time 40 mins**

   per serving

A rich, versatile Quorn and tomato sauce that can be served Bolognese-style with spaghetti or used as a base for pies and bakes.

Calorie controlled cooking spray
2 large onions, diced
4 carrots, diced
4 sticks celery, diced
600g mushrooms, sliced
4 garlic cloves, crushed
60g tomato purée
4 tablespoons balsamic vinegar

3 x 400g tins chopped tomatoes
400ml vegetable stock, made with 1 stock cube
3 teaspoons paprika
3 x 500g packs frozen Quorn mince
2 large handfuls fresh basil leaves, chopped

1   Mist your largest nonstick pan with cooking spray and cook the onion, carrot and celery over a medium heat, covered, for 15-18 minutes, until softened. Stir in the mushrooms and cook for 5 minutes, then add the garlic and cook for 1 minute.

2   Stir in the tomato purée, vinegar, tomatoes, stock and paprika. Split the mixture between 2 pans, if necessary, then stir through the Quorn in 2 batches. Season well. Bring the mixture to the boil and simmer for 10-12 minutes, before stirring in the basil. Season to taste, then set aside to cool completely before portioning and freezing.

TO FREEZE Divide the ragù equally between 3 airtight containers and freeze for up to 3 months. Defrost overnight in the fridge.

COOK'S TIP To make this vegan, use 3 x 400g packs The Meatless Farm Meat Free Mince instead of Quorn.

One
Lentil spaghetti with Quorn ragù

serves 4   **prep time 2 mins**   **cook time 10 mins**

   per serving

A saviour on days when you barely have the time to cook – this is on the table in under 15 minutes.

1 x quantity Quorn ragù, defrosted
200g WW Yellow Lentil Spaghetti
Handful fresh basil leaves, torn, to serve
60g vegetarian Italian-style hard cheese, grated, to serve

1   Reheat the Quorn ragù in a medium pan, until piping hot.

2   Meanwhile, cook the lentil spaghetti in a large pan of boiling water for 8 minutes then drain and toss through the ragù.

3   Divide between bowls and serve garnished with the basil and grated cheese.

Two
Indian-spiced Quorn ragù pot pies

serves 4 **prep time 15 mins** **cook time 45 mins**

    per serving

A touch of toasted spice stirred into the ragù brings a new flavour dimension to these pies.

1 tablespoon medium curry powder
1 x quantity Quorn ragù, defrosted
200g small Maris Piper or King Edward potatoes
150g parsnips
1 tablespoon low-fat spread, melted
320g Tenderstem broccoli

1 Heat a large nonstick pan over a medium heat and dry fry the curry powder, stirring, for 2 minutes until fragrant. Stir through the ragù and gently heat through while you prepare the topping.
2 Preheat the oven to 200°C, fan 180°C, gas mark 6.
3 Bring a large pan of salted water to the boil. Peel and slice the potatoes and parsnips into 2mm-thick slices (use a mandoline if you have one). Blanch the potatoes and parsnips in the boiling water for 2 minutes, then drain in a colander and refresh under cold running water. Lay out on a clean tea towel to dry, then season well.
4 Spoon the ragù into 4 medium ovenproof dishes. Layer the potatoes and parsnip slices on top, then brush with the melted spread and bake in the oven for 30-40 minutes until golden and crisp on top.
5 Steam the broccoli in a steamer set over a pan of boiling water for 3-5 minutes until tender, then drain and serve with the pies.

Three
Quorn ragù tortilla bake

serves 4

prep time 20 mins + cooling **cook time 40 mins**

    per serving

A deliciously different way to enjoy a Tex-Mex fave.

Calorie controlled cooking spray
1 red pepper, deseeded and diced
1 teaspoon ground cumin
1 teaspoon smoked paprika
½ teaspoon dried oregano
1 x quantity Quorn ragù, defrosted
50g pitted green olives in brine, drained and halved
3 tablespoons chopped fresh coriander, plus extra to serve

4 x WW White Wraps
100g WW Reduced Fat Grated Mature Cheese

FOR THE SALSA
4 tomatoes, chopped
2 spring onions, trimmed and chopped
1 tablespoon chopped fresh coriander
Grated zest and juice of 1 lime

1 Preheat the oven to 200°C, fan 180°C, gas mark 6. Mist a nonstick frying pan with cooking spray and cook the pepper with 2 tablespoons water for 6-8 minutes until softened. Add the cumin, paprika and oregano and cook, stirring, for 1-2 minutes. Put the ragù into a bowl and stir in the pepper mixture along with the olives and coriander, until combined.
2 Spread one-quarter of the ragù over the base of a deep 21cm round baking dish. Top with 1 of the wraps and scatter over one-quarter of the cheese. Repeat with the remaining ragù, wraps and cheese, then bake for 25-30 minutes until golden. Let cool for 5 minutes then scatter over the extra coriander.
3 Meanwhile, make a salsa. Combine all the salsa ingredients in a small bowl, then season to taste. Serve with the tortilla bake.

Three ways with...
Pork polpette

Make 48 proper pork meatballs to stash away in the freezer, then use them, one-by-one, in bakes, stir-fries and sandwiches.

Master recipe
Pork polpette

makes 48   prep time 10 mins   cook time 35 mins

    per polpette

A tasty meatball recipe that's versatile enough to be used in all kinds of dishes.

Calorie controlled cooking spray
2 onions, finely diced
3 garlic cloves, crushed
3 x 35g slices stale white bread, crusts removed
3 x 500g packs extra-lean pork mince
2 egg yolks, beaten

1   Mist a large nonstick frying pan with cooking spray and fry the onions for 5-7 minutes, stirring occasionally, until softened. Add the garlic and cook, stirring, for a further minute. Transfer to a plate and set aside to cool.

2   Preheat the oven to 200°C, fan 180°C, gas mark 6. Soak the bread in cold water for 30 seconds, then squeeze well to remove excess water and crumble it into a large bowl. Add the pork mince, egg yolks and cooled onion mixture. Mix with clean hands until combined. Season well and shape into 48 meatballs, each slightly smaller than a golf ball.

3   Put the meatballs on 2 large baking trays, mist all over with cooking spray and bake in the oven for 30-35 minutes, until browned and cooked through. Set aside to cool completely before freezing and portioning.

TO FREEZE Open freeze the meatballs on the baking trays for 1-2 hours, until solid. Divide into 3 x batches of 16 polpette and freeze in freezer bags or airtight containers for up to 3 months. Defrost overnight in the fridge.

One
Sticky hoisin pork polpette with rice

serves 4   prep time 20 mins   cook time 45 mins

    per serving

The whole family will enjoy tucking into tender juicy meatballs in a sticky, sweet hoisin glaze.

120g brown basmati rice
100g hoisin sauce
1 tablespoon rice wine vinegar
½ teaspoon clear honey
2 teaspoons finely chopped ginger
Calorie controlled cooking spray
1 garlic clove, finely sliced
3 pak choi, cut into wedges
100g mangetout
1 x quantity pork polpette (16 polpette), defrosted
1 small red chilli, deseeded and sliced (optional), to serve

1   Cook the rice in a pan of boiling water to pack instructions. Drain and keep covered until ready to serve.

2   In a small bowl, mix together the hoisin sauce, rice wine vinegar, honey, 3 tablespoons water and half the ginger. Set aside.

3   Mist a large nonstick lidded frying pan with cooking spray. Stir-fry the garlic and remaining ginger for 30 seconds over a medium heat. Add the pak choi with 3 tablespoons water. Stir, then put the lid on and steam for 4 minutes. Add the mangetout and stir-fry for a further 2 minutes, then set aside in a bowl, cover and keep warm.

4   Reduce the heat to low, then add the meatballs to the pan and cook, for 5 minutes until warmed through. Add the hoisin sauce mixture and cook, stirring, for 2 minutes, until sticky. Serve the sticky meatballs with the rice and greens, garnished with the chilli, if using.

Two
Sicilian pork polpette bake

serves 4   **prep time 25 mins**   **cook time 55 mins**

    per serving

A super-easy, family-friendly pasta bake that's loaded with meat, cheese and tomatoes.

Calorie controlled cooking spray
1 onion, sliced
2 red or yellow peppers, deseeded and sliced
2 garlic cloves, finely sliced
2 teaspoons fennel seeds
¼ teaspoon chilli flakes
500ml chicken stock, made with ½ stock cube
400g tin chopped tomatoes
Zest of 1 lemon
100g orzo
1 x quantity pork polpette (16 polpette), defrosted
125g light mozzarella, torn
20g Parmesan, grated
10g dried white breadcrumbs
Green salad, to serve

1   Mist a nonstick lidded frying pan with cooking spray and stir-fry the onions and peppers for 5 minutes over a medium heat. Add the garlic, fennel seeds and chilli and cook for 2 minutes, stirring. Pour in half the stock and cook, covered, for 5-7 minutes. Add the remaining stock and the tomatoes and cook for 10 minutes. Stir in the zest and season to taste.

2   Meanwhile, cook the orzo for 2 minutes less than the pack instructions suggest. Drain, refresh under cold running water, then drain again and set aside.

3   Preheat the oven to 200°C, fan 180°C, gas mark 6. Put the meatballs into a medium baking dish and spoon the orzo around them. Pour over the sauce and top with the mozzarella, Parmesan and breadcrumbs. Bake for 25-30 minutes then serve with the salad.

Three
Pork polpette pittas with harissa yogurt

makes 4   **prep time 10 mins**   **cook time 15 mins**

    per pitta

Pittas stuffed with meatballs, salad and a spicy harissa yogurt come together in no time at all.

1 x quantity pork polpette (16 polpette), defrosted
Calorie controlled cooking spray
4 x 60g wholemeal pitta breads
80g rocket
8 cherry tomatoes, quartered
½ small red onion, finely sliced

FOR THE HARISSA YOGURT
100g 0% fat natural Greek yogurt
¾ teaspoon harissa paste
1 teaspoon lime juice

1   Preheat the oven to 180°C, fan 160°C, gas mark 4. Put the defrosted meatballs on a baking tray, mist with cooking spray and heat for 10-15 minutes until piping hot throughout.

2   Meanwhile, make the harissa yogurt. In a small bowl, mix the yogurt with the harissa, lime juice and a small pinch of salt.

3   Warm the pittas in the oven for the final 2 minutes of the meatballs' reheating time. To serve, split the pittas and divide the rocket, cherry tomatoes and red onion between them. Put 4 meatballs into each pitta and spoon over the harissa yogurt.

Three ways with...
Fish goujons

Coating fish goujons is totally worth the effort, and with a triple batch, you only need to do it once.

Master recipe
Quinoa-crusted fish goujons

makes 36 goujons
prep time 20 minutes   cook time 20 minutes

  per goujon

Crunchy quinoa and Parmesan crust on the outside, juicy tender cod on the inside. Delicious!

180g quinoa
75g sourdough breadcrumbs
60g Parmesan, grated
75g plain flour
3 eggs, lightly beaten
1.2kg cod loin, cut into chunky strips
(you'll need 36 strips)
Calorie controlled cooking spray

1   Toast the quinoa in a dry frying pan for 4-5 minutes, until fragrant. Remove from the heat and let cool, then put into a food processor and blitz to a fine crumb. Transfer to a shallow dish, add the breadcrumbs and Parmesan and mix to combine.
2   Put the flour in a second shallow bowl and season well, then put the eggs into a third shallow bowl. Dip the fish first in the flour, then in the egg and finally in the quinoa crumb. Transfer to a large baking tray that's misted with calorie controlled cooking spray.

TO FREEZE Flash freeze the fish goujons on the baking tray, for 1-2 hours until firm, then divide into 3 x batches of 12 goujons and freeze in freezer bags or an airtight container for up to 3 months.

TO COOK To cook from fresh, preheat the oven to 210°C, fan 190°C, gas mark 7. Mist the goujons all over with cooking spray and bake for 14-16 minutes, turning halfway through, until cooked and golden.

One
Crispy fish tacos with lime slaw & mango salsa

serves 4   prep time 15 mins   cook time 30 mins

  per serving

Soft corn tortillas stuffed with crunchy fish goujons, zesty slaw and a sweet and hot salsa.

1 x quantity frozen quinoa-crusted fish goujons (12 goujons)
Calorie controlled cooking spray
4 x 42g corn tortillas (we used Old El Paso)

FOR THE LIME SLAW
100g white cabbage, shredded
100g red cabbage, shredded

1 carrot, grated
Juice of 1 lime
75g lighter than light mayonnaise (we used Hellmann's)
Handful of fresh coriander

FOR THE MANGO SALSA
1 small mango, finely diced
100g cherry tomatoes, finely diced
1 red chilli, finely diced
Zest and juice of 1 lime

1   Preheat the oven to 200°C, fan 180°C, gas mark 6. Put the goujons on a baking sheet and mist all over with cooking spray. Bake for 30 minutes, or until cooked through and golden.
2   To make the slaw, mix the cabbages and carrot together in a large bowl. Add the remaining slaw ingredients and stir to combine. Season to taste.
3   To make the mango salsa, combine all of the salsa ingredients in a small bowl, then set aside.
4   Just before serving, warm the tortillas on a hot griddle pan. Divide the slaw between the tortillas, then top each with the goujons and mango salsa.

Two
Fish goujons with Mexican-style rice

serves 4 **prep time 10 mins** **cook time 30 mins**

   per serving

Charred corn kernels and crumbled feta take this Mexican-style rice to another level.

1 x quantity frozen quinoa-crusted fish goujons (12 goujons)
Calorie controlled cooking spray
2 corn on the cob
Handful fresh coriander
45g light feta, crumbled
Sliced jalapeños in brine, drained, to serve (optional)

FOR THE MEXICAN-STYLE RICE
240g brown basmati rice
1 red onion, finely sliced
1 garlic clove, finely sliced
1 teaspoon dried oregano
1 teaspoon smoked paprika
3 Romano peppers, deseeded and thickly sliced
150g young leaf spinach

1 Preheat the oven to 200°C, fan 180°C, gas mark 6. Put the goujons on a baking sheet and mist all over with cooking spray. Bake for 30 minutes, or until cooked through and golden.

2 Meanwhile, make the Mexican-style rice. Cook the rice to pack instructions, then drain and set aside. At the same time, mist a nonstick frying pan with cooking spray and fry the onion for 6-8 minutes. Add the garlic, oregano and paprika and cook for 2 minutes. Add the peppers and a splash of water and cook for 8-10 minutes. Stir in the cooked rice, then add the spinach, cover, and let wilt. Season.

3 Meanwhile, cook the corn in a pan of boiling water for 4-5 minutes, then drain and set aside. Mist the corn with cooking spray, cook on a hot griddle until starting to char, then cut the kernels from the cobs.

4 Serve the fish with the rice and corn, garnished with the feta, coriander and jalapeños, if using.

Three
Fish goujons with crushed ricotta peas

serves 4 **prep time 15 mins** **cook time 30 mins**

   per serving

Use your goujons to scoop up the ricotta peas – a sophisticated take on the classic mushy pea side.

1 x quantity frozen quinoa-crusted fish goujons (12 goujons)
Calorie controlled cooking spray
50g pea shoots

FOR THE CRUSHED RICOTTA PEAS
400g peas, fresh or frozen
1 garlic clove, finely chopped

125g ricotta
Zest and juice of 1 lemon
Handful of fresh mint

FOR THE PICKLED RED ONIONS
75ml apple cider vinegar
1 tablespoon light brown sugar
1 teaspoon sea salt
2 red onions, finely sliced

1 To make the pickled red onions, whisk the vinegar, sugar and salt together in a small bowl. Add the onions, cover and set aside to 'pickle' for at least 15 minutes.

2 Preheat the oven to 200°C, fan 180°C, gas mark 6. Put the goujons on a baking sheet and mist all over with cooking spray. Bake for 30 minutes, or until cooked through and golden.

3 Meanwhile, make the crushed ricotta peas. Cook the peas in a pan of boiling water for 3-4 minutes, then drain and refresh under cold water. Drain again and set aside. Put the garlic, ricotta, lemon zest and juice and half of the mint in a food processor. Add two-thirds of the peas and blitz to a chunky purée. Season then stir in the remaining peas and mint.

4 Drain the onions from the pickling liquid and toss them with the pea shoots. Divide between plates and serve with the fish goujons and crushed peas.

Three ways with...
Kale pesto

For minimum effort and maximum flavour, you can't beat homemade pesto.
It's perfect for storing in your freezer to use as and when you need it.

Master recipe
Kale pesto

serves 12　prep time 15 mins　cook time 5 mins

   per serving

For a pesto that packs a powerful nutritional punch, whizz up a batch of leafy green kale with the usual fresh, fragrant basil.

400g shredded kale
30g bunch basil (leaves and stalks)
150g vegetarian Italian-style hard cheese, grated
4 garlic cloves, roughly chopped
3 tablespoons olive oil
5 tablespoons lemon juice

1 In 2 batches, blanch the kale for 1 minute in a large pan of salted, boiling water. Drain in a colander and refresh under cold running water. Squeeze out the excess water with your hands.
2 Put the blanched kale and remaining ingredients into a food processor and whizz to a chunky pesto. Season to taste before portioning and freezing.

TO FREEZE Divide the pesto equally between 3 airtight containers and freeze for up to 1 month. Defrost overnight at room temperature.

COOK'S TIP You can also use Parmesan in this recipe – the SmartPoints will remain the same but the pesto will no longer be vegetarian.

One
Fusilli with kale pesto & tomatoes

serves 4　prep time 5 mins　cook time 15 mins

   per serving

This easy pasta dish is just as delicious served cold for lunch the next day.

240g wholewheat fusilli
1 x quantity kale pesto, defrosted
250g vine cherry tomatoes, halved
Handful rocket leaves

1 Cook the fusilli in a large pan of salted boiling water to pack instructions. Drain, reserving 2 ladlefuls of the pasta cooking water, then return the pasta to the pan.
2 Stir through the pesto, adding just enough of the reserved cooking water to give a coating consistency, then toss through the tomatoes and rocket. Divide between bowls and serve.

Two
Chicken, mushroom & kale pesto pizza

serves 4   prep time 15 mins   cook time 30 mins

   per serving

Spread the pesto over the base of your pizza instead of tomato sauce – you won't look back!

3 x 165g skinless chicken breast fillets, cut into thin strips
Calorie controlled cooking spray
300g chestnut mushrooms, sliced
1 x quantity kale pesto, defrosted
4 x 65g wholemeal flatbreads (we used Crosta & Mollica Piadina flatbreads)
100g light mozzarella, grated
Small handful basil leaves

1   Preheat the oven to 200°C, fan 180°C, gas mark 6. Line 2 large baking trays with baking paper.
2   Season the chicken. Mist a large nonstick frying pan with cooking spray and cook the chicken over a high heat for 2-3 minutes on each side, or until golden and cooked through – you'll need to do this in 2 batches. Transfer to a plate and set aside.
3   Mist the pan with more cooking spray and fry the mushrooms, with seasoning, over a medium heat for 5 minutes until browned. Remove from the heat.
4   Put the flatbreads on the prepared baking trays then thinly spread the pesto over the 4 flatbreads, leaving a 1-2cm border. Top with the chicken and mushrooms. Scatter over the mozzarella and bake for 10-12 minutes. Serve garnished with the basil.

Three
Pesto chicken cobbler

serves 4   prep time 20 mins   cook time 55 mins

   per serving

A hearty, filling dish that has year-round appeal – serve it simply with a salad on the side.

Calorie controlled cooking spray
2 shallots, finely sliced
3 leeks, trimmed and sliced
600ml chicken stock, made with 1 stock cube
4 x 165g skinless chicken breast fillets
25g cornflour
30g half-fat crème fraîche
1 x quantity kale pesto, defrosted
125g plain flour
1 teaspoon baking powder
½ teaspoon fine salt
1 egg, beaten
75ml buttermilk
1 tablespoon finely chopped fresh chives
60g mixed salad leaves, to serve

1   Mist a large nonstick pan with cooking spray and fry the shallots and leeks over a medium heat, covered, for 6-8 minutes, stirring occasionally, until softened. Set aside on a plate.
2   Put the stock and chicken into the same pan, and bring to a simmer. Season and simmer gently for 15 minutes. Remove from the heat and leave the chicken to cool in the stock for 10 minutes, before lifting out onto a plate with a slotted spoon.
3   Preheat the oven to 200°C, fan 180°C, gas mark 6. Bring the stock up to the boil. Combine the cornflour with 3 tablespoons water then whisk it into the stock, until thickened. Simmer for 5 minutes then remove from the heat and stir in the cooked veg, crème fraîche and pesto. Shred the chicken and stir through the sauce, then tip into a medium baking dish.
4   For the cobbler topping, combine the flour, baking powder, salt, egg, buttermilk and chives in a bowl and bring together to a sticky dough. Spoon 4 large spoonfuls of the dough over the chicken mixture. Bake for 18-20 minutes until the topping is risen and golden. Serve with the salad.

Three ways with...
Greek yogurt cake

Having a ready-made stash of homemade cakes in
the freezer, plus a selection of easy decorating ideas,
is bound to make you feel more relaxed about any
last-minute gatherings or guests...

Master recipe
Greek yogurt cake

makes 3 cakes (serves 36)
prep time 10 mins   cook time 1 hour

    per serving

Delicious and moist, this superb loaf cake recipe is a great one to have in your repertoire.

Calorie controlled cooking spray
400g caster sugar
225g low-fat spread
9 eggs
500g low-fat natural Greek yogurt (we used Tesco)
1 tablespoon vanilla extract
525g self-raising flour, sifted

1   Preheat the oven to 180°C, fan 160°C, gas mark 4. Mist 3 x 450g loaf tins with cooking spray and line with baking paper.

2   Put the sugar and low-fat spread into a large mixing bowl and beat together until well combined. Add the eggs, one at a time, beating well between each addition, then fold in the yogurt and vanilla until fully incorporated.

3   Sift the flour into the mixture and carefully fold through. Divide between the prepared tins and bake for 50 minutes to 1 hour until risen and golden and a skewer inserted into the centre of the cakes comes out clean.

4   Leave the cooked cakes to cool in the tins for 10 minutes, before turning out onto a wire rack to cool completely.

TO FREEZE Wrap the cooled cakes in clingfilm, then kitchen foil and freeze for up to 4 months. Defrost at room temperature before decorating and serving.

One
Lemon meringue pie cake

serves 12   prep time 10 minutes

   per serving

All the flavours of a lemon meringue pie, without having to go to the trouble of making one!

150g 0% fat natural Greek yogurt, well chilled
½ tablespoon agave syrup
2 tablespoons lemon curd
25g ready-made meringues, broken into pieces
1 Greek yogurt cake, defrosted

1   Put the yogurt into a small bowl and whisk in the agave syrup, swirl through half of the lemon curd and half the meringue pieces.

2   Spread the mixture over the top of the cake, then swirl with the remaining lemon curd, and scatter over the remaining meringue pieces.

Two
Strawberry syrup cake

serves 12
prep time 10 mins + cooling   cook time 5 mins

  **7 7 7** per serving

A fruity topping that tastes as good as it looks.

400g strawberries, hulled and quartered
3 tablespoons agave syrup
150g 0% fat natural Greek yogurt
100g medium-fat soft cheese
1 Greek yogurt cake, defrosted

1 To make a strawberry compote, put half of the strawberries in a pan with half of the agave syrup and 2 tablespoons water. Bring to a boil over a medium heat, then reduce to a simmer and cook for 5 minutes, or until the strawberries have broken down completely. Use a hand blender to blitz to a purée, then pass the mixture through a fine sieve. Set aside to cool completely.

2 In a bowl, whisk together the yogurt, soft cheese and remaining agave syrup, then spread over the top of the cake, using a palette knife.

3 Decorate the top of the cake with the remaining strawberries, then drizzle over the compote.

Three
Orange & pistachio cake

serves 12   prep time 10 mins   cook time 5 mins

  8 8 8 per serving

Sticky, candied orange zest and crunchy pistachio kernels work brilliantly well together.

1 orange
1 tablespoon agave syrup
75g icing sugar
1 Greek yogurt cake, defrosted
30g pistachio kernels, roughly chopped

1 Pare off some long, thin strips of zest from the orange, then cut the zest into very thin strips. Juice the orange and set aside.

2 Put the agave into a small pan with 1 tablespoon water and slowly bring to a simmer. Add the pared orange zest and simmer for 2-3 minutes. Remove the peel from the liquid and set aside on a wire rack to dry out.

3 Sift the icing sugar into a bowl and add 1 tablespoon of the orange juice. Stir to combine, adding more orange juice, if needed, to reach a drizzling consistency.

4 Drizzle the icing over the top of the cake, then scatter over the candied orange zest and chopped pistachios.

Batch bakes & frozen desserts

74 **Cinnamon & raisin swirl buns**

76 **Pear & blueberry crumbles**

78 **Cheesecake swirl brownies**

80 **Ginger & oat biscuits**

82 **Carrot cake ice lollies**

84 **Frozen tiramisu slice**

86 **Caramel cluster fro-yo**

88 **Almond & cherry oat bars**

90 **Lemon & yogurt pancakes**

92 **Cheese & Marmite English muffins**

94 **Beetroot & goat's cheese tarts**

96 **Mediterranean muffins**

    Cheese & broccoli muffins

    Bircher muesli muffins

    Rhubarb & custard muffins

Cinnamon & raisin swirl buns

makes 12   **prep time 40 minutes + rising**   **cook time 30 minutes**

  per bun

These Scandi-style cinnamon-spiced buns are delicious served straight from the oven, or warmed in the microwave later down the line.

200ml skimmed milk

75g low-fat spread

125g white spelt flour

300g plain flour, plus 10g extra for dusting

1 teaspoon ground cinnamon

½ teaspoon salt

50g granulated sugar

10g dried yeast

1 egg, lightly beaten

Calorie controlled cooking spray

FOR THE FILLING

75g low-fat spread

25g granulated sugar

2 teaspoons ground cinnamon

1 teaspoon vanilla extract

25g raisins

TO FINISH

1 egg, lightly beaten

5g demerara sugar

1   Heat the milk until just below boiling point, then stir in the low-fat spread to melt. Set aside until it reaches 38°C. In a bowl, sift the flours, cinnamon and salt, then stir in the sugar and yeast. Make a well, add the egg then stir in the milk until a sticky dough forms (see Cook's tip).

2   Dust a surface with the extra 10g flour, then scrape the dough out onto it; knead for 5 minutes until smooth. Mist the bowl with cooking spray and return the dough to it. Cover and set aside in a warm place for 1 hour until doubled in size. Tip out onto the floured surface, knock out the air and roll out to a 25cm x 35cm rectangle.

3   Meanwhile, prepare the filling. Use a hand-held electric whisk to beat together the spread, sugar, cinnamon and vanilla in a bowl until combined, then set aside.

4   Grease and line 2 x 20cm round cake tins with baking paper. Spread the filling over the dough, then scatter over the raisins. Starting from a long edge, roll the dough up tightly like a swiss roll. Cut into 12 slices and arrange, cut-side up, in the prepared tins. Cover and leave to rise for 20-30 minutes.

5   Preheat the oven to 200°C, fan 180°C, gas mark 6. Brush the buns with the beaten egg, sprinkle over the demerara sugar and bake for 25 minutes, until golden.

Cook's tip
The dough is very wet, but persevere as it will come together – don't be tempted to add more flour! If you haven't any spelt flour, use the same quantity of regular flour.

To store
The buns will keep in an airtight container at room temperature for up to 2 days.

To freeze
Wrap the buns in clingfilm, followed by foil and freeze for up to 4 months. Defrost at room temperature and warm in the microwave to serve.

Pear & blueberry crumbles

makes 6   **prep time 10 minutes**   **cook time 20 minutes**

  5 per crumble

A simple fruit-and-vanilla pud made extra special with a crunchy hazelnut topping that's sweetened with rich, sticky maple syrup.

Calorie controlled cooking spray

5 pears, peeled, cored and cut into small chunks (you'll need 400g prepared weight)

200g blueberries

2 teaspoons vanilla extract

1 teaspoon maple syrup

FOR THE CRUMBLE

30g plain flour

50g low-fat spread, chilled

80g porridge oats

30g blanched hazelnuts, chopped

60ml maple syrup

1 To make the crumble, put the flour into a bowl, add the low-fat spread and rub together using your fingertips until clumps form. Add the oats and hazelnuts and stir to combine, then stir in the maple syrup until everything is well combined. Chill in the fridge while you prep the filling.

2 Mist 6 x 250ml ramekins with cooking spray. In a medium bowl, mix together the pears, blueberries, vanilla and maple syrup. Divide the mixture between the prepared ramekins, then spoon over the chilled crumble filling.

Cook's tip
If you don't like maple syrup, use the same quantities of agave syrup or honey instead. Just remember to adjust the SmartPoints.

To serve
Preheat the oven to 200°C, fan 180°C, gas mark 6. Put the ramekins on a baking tray and cook in the oven for 20 minutes, or until the filling is bubbling and the crumble topping is crisp and golden. Remove from the oven and let cool slightly before serving.

To freeze
Wrap the uncooked crumbles in kitchen foil and freeze for up to 3 months. Keep the foil covering on and cook from frozen in an oven that's preheated to 200°C, fan 180°C, gas mark 6 for 20 minutes, then remove the foil and cook for a further 15-20 minutes, until the filling is piping hot and the crumble is golden.

Cheesecake swirl brownies

makes 16   prep time 40 minutes   cook time 20 minutes

   per brownie bar

A show-stopping bake that's sure to impress. White chocolate cheesecake filling is swirled though a fudgy chocolate brownie base, then studded with fresh, juicy raspberries.

Calorie controlled cooking spray

40g tinned black beans, drained and rinsed

2 eggs, plus 1 egg white

1 teaspoon vanilla extract

85g dark chocolate (54% cocoa solids)

40g low-fat spread

160g caster sugar

100g plain flour

20g cocoa powder

½ teaspoon baking powder

½ teaspoon salt

16 large raspberries, halved

FOR THE CHEESECAKE TOPPING

30g white chocolate

20g caster sugar

½ teaspoon vanilla extract

1 egg yolk

160g medium-fat soft cheese, at room temperature

1 To make the cheesecake topping, put the white chocolate in a microwave-safe bowl and microwave on High until melted. Set aside to cool, then whisk in the remaining ingredients. Cover and chill in the fridge until needed.

2 Preheat the oven to 180°C, fan 160°C, gas mark 4. Mist a shallow 30cm x 17cm baking tin with cooking spray, and line with baking paper.

3 To make the brownie base, put the black beans, eggs, egg white and vanilla into a mini food processor. Blitz until smooth, then transfer to a bowl and set aside. Put the chocolate and low-fat spread in a microwave-safe bowl and microwave on High until melted. Let cool. Whisk in the sugar then stir this into the black bean mixture.

4 In a separate bowl, sift together the flour, cocoa powder, baking powder and salt. Gently fold this mixture into the chocolate mixture until smooth and combined, then spread it into the prepared tin.

5 Dot the cheesecake mixture over the brownie base and use a knife to swirl through to create a marbled effect. Press the raspberries into the top and bake for 15-16 minutes until just set. Leave to cool in the tin before cutting into 16 bars.

Cook's tip
For a more intense raspberry flavour, stir some chopped fresh raspberries through the brownie base mixture in Step 4. The SmartPoints will remain the same.

To store
The brownie bars will keep in an airtight container in the fridge for up to 3 days.

To freeze
Wrap in clingfilm, followed by foil and freeze for up to 4 months. Defrost at room temperature.

Ginger & oat biscuits

makes 16   prep time 15 minutes   cook time 15 minutes

   per biscuit

These fuss-free biscuits are so quick and easy to make and will keep well – they're the perfect partner for your afternoon cuppa.

125g self-raising flour

1½ teaspoons ground ginger

½ teaspoon fine salt

60g demerara sugar

40g porridge oats

100g low-fat spread

1   Preheat the oven to 180°C, fan 160°C, gas mark 4. Line 2 baking trays with baking paper.

2   Sift the flour and ginger into a mixing bowl then stir in the salt, sugar and porridge oats. Add the low-fat spread and, using a wooden spoon, mix well to bring the ingredients together into a sticky ball of dough.

3   Use a tablespoon measure to create 16 small balls of dough and space them out on the prepared trays. Press each one down with the back of a fork into discs with a thickness of about 1cm.

4   Bake for 14-15 minutes until the biscuits are a light golden brown, turning the tray around halfway through cooking so that they colour evenly.

5   Cool on the tray until set, then transfer to a wire rack to cool completely.

Cook's tip
Add 50g raisins along with the porridge oats in Step 2. The SmartPoints will be the same.

To store
The biscuits will keep in an airtight container at room temperature for up to 1 week.

To freeze
Layer the biscuits between sheets of baking paper and freeze in an airtight container or freezer bag for up to 3 months. Defrost at room temperature.

Carrot cake ice lollies

makes 12   prep time 20 minutes + cooling and freezing   cook time 5 minutes

   per ice lolly

Everything you love about a classic carrot cake packed into individual icy treats.

40g pecans

400g coarsely grated carrot (prepared weight)

600g roughly chopped fresh pineapple

3 tablespoons agave syrup

220g medium-fat soft cheese

90ml freshly squeezed orange juice

1 teaspoon ground mixed spice

½ teaspoon ground cinnamon

1   Preheat the oven to 180°C, fan 160°C, gas mark 4. Put the pecans on a small baking tray and toast for 8-10 minutes until golden. Set aside to cool, then chop.

2   Put the carrot in a microwave-safe bowl, cover and microwave on High for 3 minutes to soften. Let cool.

3   In a food processor, blitz the cooled carrot with the pineapple, agave syrup, soft cheese, orange juice and spices until smooth.

4   Divide the toasted pecans between 12 x 100ml ice-lolly moulds. Pour the carrot mixture into the moulds and insert ice-lolly sticks. Freeze for at least 4 hours or overnight until firm.

Cook's tip
Try making these in WW Ice Lolly Moulds, available from the online shop.

To serve
To easily unmould the ice lollies, fill a jug with warm water and briefly dip the moulds in to loosen – about 20-30 seconds.

To freeze
The ice lollies will keep in the freezer for up to 2 months.

Frozen tiramisu slice

serves 10   prep time 20 minutes + cooling, freezing and standing

   per serving

Our frozen version of the classic Italian dessert is the perfect thing to slice and serve after dinner with friends.

5g instant coffee granules

3 tablespoons agave syrup

180g medium-fat soft cheese

3 tablespoons Marsala or sweet sherry

375g fat-free vanilla yogurt (we used Onken)

160g Madeira sponge cake (we used Sainsbury's), trimmed from a 275g cake

1   Line a 500g loaf tin (approximately 20cm x 11cm x 7cm) with clingfilm, allowing a 5cm overhang. Combine the coffee and 2 teaspoons of the agave syrup in a heatproof bowl. Add 75ml boiling water from the kettle and stir until the coffee dissolves. Set aside to cool.

2   Using a hand-held electric whisk, beat the soft cheese, Marsala and remaining agave syrup in a bowl until smooth. Beat in 1 tablespoon of the coffee mixture, then fold in the yogurt until combined.

3   Ensure the top of the sponge has a flat surface. Cut the cake horizontally into 4 x 1cm-thick slices and brush liberally with the remaining coffee mixture. Spread half of the cream cheese mixture into the prepared tin. Top with a layer of sponge, coffee-side down, trimming to fit. Repeat with the remaining cream cheese mixture and sponge. Cover and freeze overnight.

Cook's tip
This is a good dessert to serve whole at a large gathering. Dust the top with 1 tablespoon cocoa powder and 30g shaved dark chocolate before serving.

To serve
Lift the tiramisu from the tin and place, cake-side down, on a board. Stand at room temperature for 10-15 minutes, then cut as many slices as you need. Put the tiramisu back in the tin, cover and return to the freezer.

To freeze
The tiramisu slice will keep in the freezer for up to 1 month.

Caramel cluster fro-yo

serves 12   prep time 10 minutes + churning and freezing   cook time 10 minutes

   per serving

Tangy yogurt and swirls of rich caramel sauce are a flavour match made in heaven. For added caramel flavour and crunch, we've stirred through WW Caramel Clusters.

750g 0% fat natural Greek yogurt

150g caster sugar

2 teaspoons vanilla extract

6 WW Chocolate Caramel Clusters, broken into small chunks

FOR THE CARAMEL SAUCE

50g caster sugar

20g low-fat spread

30ml single cream alternative (we used Elmlea)

1   Put the yogurt, sugar and vanilla into a bowl and whisk, using a hand-held electric whisk, until the sugar is dissolved. Chill in the fridge for 1 hour.

2   Meanwhile, make the caramel sauce. Put the sugar in a small, heavy-based pan and heat over a medium heat until the sugar is completely melted and turns an amber colour. Reduce the heat to low, stir in the low-fat spread and let the mixture boil for 1-2 minutes, until melted and combined. Add the cream alternative and bubble for 1 minute, then remove from the heat and set aside to cool.

3   Put the chilled yogurt mixture into the bowl of an ice cream maker (see Cook's tip) and churn for 30 minutes, or to manufacturer's instructions, until the mixture reaches a soft-serve consistency. Transfer half the mixture to a freezer-safe container, drizzle over half the caramel sauce and half the caramel clusters, then use a knife to create a swirl. Repeat with the remaining frozen yogurt, caramel and caramel clusters. Cover and return to the freezer.

Cook's tip
If you don't have an ice cream maker, pour the yogurt mixture into a freezer-safe container and freeze for 2 hours. Break up the semi-frozen mixture, put it into the bowl of a food processor and process until smooth. Return to the freezer and repeat the process until smooth. Add the caramel sauce and clusters as per Step 3 and return to the freezer to freeze completely.

To serve
Remove from the freezer 30 minutes before you plan to serve, to allow the frozen yogurt to reach a scooping consistency. Serve 80g per person.

To freeze
The frozen yogurt will keep in the freezer for up to 3 months.

Almond & cherry oat bars

makes 16   **prep time 15 minutes**   **cook time 25 minutes**

  per oat bar

Whether packed for a picnic, slipped into a lunch box or stashed in a pocket ahead of a long walk, these chewy, fruity oat bars are the ultimate on-the-go snack.

125g wholemeal flour

60g porridge oats

50g toasted flaked almonds

1 teaspoon ground cinnamon

½ teaspoon baking powder

¼ teaspoon bicarbonate of soda

¼ teaspoon fine salt

100g dark brown soft sugar

45ml olive oil

2 large egg whites

40g almond butter
(we used Biona Organic)

1 teaspoon vanilla extract

175g fresh or frozen pitted
cherries, halved

1   Preheat the oven to 190°C, fan 170°C, gas mark 5. Line a 20cm square baking tin with baking paper, allowing the paper to rise above the edges of the tin.

2   In a large bowl, mix together the flour, oats, almonds, cinnamon, baking powder, bicarbonate of soda and salt. In another bowl, stir together the brown sugar, oil, egg whites, almond butter and vanilla extract, until combined. Add the brown sugar mixture to the flour mixture and stir well to combine. Fold through the cherries. Spoon the mixture into the prepared baking tin and spread evenly with a spatula.

3   Bake for 25 minutes or until golden brown and a skewer inserted into the centre of the bake comes out clean. Leave to cool completely in the tin on a wire rack. Lift from the tin with the aid of the paper, then cut lengthwise into 4 strips. Cut each strip into 4 squares.

Cook's tip
You could also make these bars with fresh blueberries or peeled and chopped fresh peaches instead of the cherries.

To store
The bars will keep at room temperature in an airtight container for up to 4 days.

To freeze
Layer the bars between sheets of baking paper and freeze in an airtight container or freezer bag for up to 2 months. Defrost at room temperature.

Lemon & yogurt pancakes

serves 8 (makes 16 pancakes)   **prep time 15 minutes**   **cook time 35 minutes**

  per serving

Perfect for stashing in the freezer for days when you suddenly fancy pancakes – this make-and-freeze stack is ready in a flash.

180g wholemeal flour

1 teaspoon baking powder

½ teaspoon bicarbonate of soda

½ teaspoon fine salt

3 large eggs

300ml semi-skimmed milk

100g 0% fat natural Greek yogurt

60g clear honey

2 tablespoons rapeseed oil

½ teaspoon vanilla extract

Zest of 1 lemon

Calorie controlled cooking spray

1 Mix together the flour, baking powder, bicarbonate of soda and salt in a large bowl.

2 In a separate bowl, whisk together the eggs, milk, yogurt, honey, oil, vanilla extract and lemon zest until smooth. Add the egg mixture to the flour mixture and stir until just blended.

3 Mist a nonstick frying pan with the cooking spray and set over a medium-low heat. Fill a ladle two-thirds full of the batter and pour onto the pan. Tilt the pan so that the batter spreads as thinly as possible. Cook for 1-2 minutes until one side is lightly golden then turn the pancake and cook for another 30 seconds to 1 minute. Slide it onto a plate then repeat with the remaining batter, misting the pan with more cooking spray as necessary, to make a total of 16 pancakes.

Cook's tip
Boost the fruit content by stirring fresh blueberries through the pancake batter at the end of Step 2. The SmartPoints will remain the same.

To serve
Serve 2 pancakes per person topped with 25g 0% fat natural Greek yogurt, a handful of fresh blueberries, some pared lemon zest and ½ teaspoon clear honey.

To freeze
Let the pancakes cool completely, then layer between squares of baking paper. Wrap pairs of pancakes (or a complete stack) in kitchen foil and freeze for up to 2 months. Defrost at room temperature, then reheat the foil-wrapped pancakes in an oven that's preheated to 180°C, fan 160°C, gas mark 4, for around 10 minutes.

Cheese & Marmite English muffins

makes 12   prep time 30 minutes + rising   cook time 20 minutes

  per muffin

Making English muffins from scratch is easier than you might think. Served toasted with some spread or as a base for eggs Benedict, these flavoured muffins are sure to please.

500g plain flour

1 teaspoon fine salt

2½ teaspoons dried yeast

10g nutritional yeast flakes

100g WW Reduced Fat Grated Mature Cheese

350ml skimmed milk

1 tablespoon Marmite

Calorie controlled cooking spray

20g polenta

1 Put 450g of the flour in large bowl with the salt, yeast and nutritional yeast flakes. Stir in the cheese and set aside. Warm the milk over a low heat until just below boiling. Remove from the heat; stir in the Marmite to dissolve. Set aside to cool to a temperature of 38°C.

2 Stir 300ml of the milk mixture into the flour mixture until a dough forms. If it's dry, add more milk, and if it's wet, add more flour. Dust a surface with flour, then tip out the dough. Knead for 5 minutes. Mist the bowl with cooking spray, return the dough then cover and set aside in a warm place for 1 hour to double in size.

3 Knock the dough back, then roll it out to a thickness of 1cm, then use an 8cm cookie cutter to stamp out 12 rounds, re-rolling the trimmings as you go. Scatter half the polenta on a sheet of baking paper. Put the muffins on top, and scatter over the remaining polenta. Allow to rise for 10-15 minutes.

4 Heat 2 nonstick frying pans over a medium heat. Transfer 3 muffins to each pan, then reduce the heat to low and cook for 10 minutes. Once golden on the bottom, flip the muffins and cook on the other side for 10 minutes, until the muffins sound hollow when you tap the base. Repeat with the remaining muffins.

Cook's tip

Split 1 muffin, spread with 1 teaspoon low-fat spread followed by 1 teaspoon Marmite. Top with 10g WW Reduced Fat Grated Mature Cheese and grill.

To store

The muffins will keep at room temperature in an airtight container for up to 3 days.

To freeze

Freeze in an airtight container or freezer bag for up to 4 months. Defrost at room temperature.

Beetroot & goat's cheese tarts

makes 8   prep time 30 minutes   cook time 40 minutes

   per tart

These freeform tarts, layered with earthy beetroot, tangy goat's cheese and a creamy quiche-like filling, look fantasic and are easy to assemble.

400g whole beetroot, trimmed, peeled and cut into thin rounds

3 sprigs fresh thyme

Calorie controlled cooking spray

FOR THE PASTRY

170g white spelt flour, plus an extra 10g flour for dusting

100g low-fat spread

Pinch salt

1 egg yolk

FOR THE FILLING

75g spinach

3 eggs

75g reduced-fat soured cream

75g fat-free cottage cheese

1 teaspoon thyme leaves

100g medium-fat soft goat's cheese

1 To make the pastry, put the flour, low-fat spread and salt into a food processor and blitz until combined. Add the egg yolk and blitz again until a dough ball forms. Divide into 8 balls, cover, and chill in the fridge.

2 Preheat the oven to 220°C, fan 200°C, gas mark 7. Line a roasting tin with kitchen foil, then add the beetroot and thyme sprigs. Mist with cooking spray, season and toss to coat. Roast for 15-20 minutes, until just tender.

3 Meanwhile, put the spinach in a colander set over the sink and pour over boiling water from the kettle to wilt. Drain, then squeeze out any liquid. Whisk together 2 of the eggs with the soured cream and cottage cheese. Stir in the spinach and thyme. Season and set aside.

4 Reduce the oven to 200°C, fan 180°C, gas mark 6. Roll each dough ball out on a lightly floured surface to a 12cm circle and transfer to 2 nonstick baking trays.

5 Arrange half the beetroot on each pastry circle, leaving a 2cm border, then top with the filling and remaining beetroot. Fold the pastry rims up and over the edge of the filling. Beat the remaining egg and brush it over the pastry edges. Bake for 20 minutes, then crumble over the goat's cheese and bake for a final 5-10 minutes.

Cook's tip
If you don't have spelt flour, you can use the same quantity of plain white flour instead.

To serve
Scatter over a few sprigs of fresh thyme, season with freshly ground black pepper and serve with mixed green salad leaves on the side.

To freeze
Let cool completely, then wrap the individual tarts in foil and freeze for up to 3 months. To reheat, keep the foil covering on and reheat from frozen in an oven that's preheated to 200°C, fan 180°C, gas mark 6, until piping hot.

Batch-cook muffins

Whether you prefer them sweet or savoury, for breakfast or a snack, batches of fluffy muffins that can be stored individually in the freezer always go down a treat.

Mediterranean muffins

makes 8   prep time 15 mins   cook time 25 mins

   per muffin

Preheat the oven to 200°C, fan 180°C, gas mark 6, and mist 8 x WW 2 in 1 Mini Cake Moulds with **calorie controlled cooking spray**. In a bowl, combine 180g **plain flour**, 2 teaspoons **baking powder** and ½ teaspoon **salt**. In a jug, whisk together 150ml **skimmed milk**, 3 tablespoons **olive oil** and 2 **eggs**. Add the wet ingredients to the dry ingredients; stir until combined, being careful not to overmix. Fold in 100g chopped **light feta**, 70g chopped **sundried tomatoes**, 60g sliced **pitted black olives**, and 2 tablespoons chopped **fresh basil**. Divide the batter evenly between the prepared moulds, then scatter over 50g chopped light feta. Bake for 20-25 minutes, or until risen and golden.

TO STORE Keep the muffins in an airtight container for up to 2 days, or wrap and freeze individually for up to 1 month. Defrost at room temperature.

Cheese & broccoli muffins

makes 8   prep time 15 mins   cook time 25 mins

   per muffin

Preheat the oven to 200°C, fan 180°C, gas mark 6, and mist 8 x WW 2 in 1 Mini Cake Moulds with **calorie controlled cooking spray**. Place 100g **young leaf spinach** in a colander and pour over boiling water from the kettle to wilt. Squeeze out any excess water then chop and set aside. Put 80g **broccoli** florets into a microwave-safe bowl, cover and microwave on High for 2 minutes. Drain and chop larger ones into smaller pieces. Fry 2 chopped **spring onions** and 1 crushed **garlic** clove in a frying pan misted with cooking spray, for 1-2 minutes, then remove from the heat. Beat 130ml **semi-skimmed milk**, 2 **eggs** and 2 tablespoons **olive oil** together in a bowl. Add 150g **plain flour**, 1½ teaspoons **baking powder**, ½ teaspoon **salt** and 1 tablespoon chopped **fresh chives**; stir until just combined. Fold in the spring onions, spinach, broccoli and 130g **WW Reduced Fat Grated Mature Cheese**. Spoon into the prepared moulds, scatter with an extra 20g WW Reduced-fat Grated Mature Cheese and bake for 20-25 minutes.

TO STORE Keep the muffins in an airtight container for up to 2 days, or wrap and freeze individually for up to 1 month. Defrost at room temperature.

Bircher muesli muffins

makes 12   prep time 20 mins   cook time 25 mins

   per muffin

Preheat the oven to 180°C, fan 160°C, gas mark 4. Line a 12-hole muffin tin with paper cases. In a bowl, combine 250g **wholemeal self-raising flour**, 125g **porridge oats**, 50g **light brown soft sugar**, 1 teaspoon **ground cinnamon**, 2 teaspoons **baking powder** and a pinch of **salt**. Stir through 1 grated **apple** and 125g **raspberries**. In a large jug, whisk together 2 **eggs**, 140g **fat-free vanilla yogurt** (we used Onken) and 125ml **buttermilk**. Stir this through the flour mixture. Divide the mixture between the paper cases and scatter over 5g **pumpkin seeds**, 10g **sunflower seeds** and 2 tablespoons porridge oats (optional). Bake for 20–25 minutes or until risen and golden.

TO STORE Keep the muffins in an airtight container for up to 2 days, or wrap and freeze individually for up to 1 month. Defrost at room temperature.

Rhubarb & custard muffins

makes 8   prep time 15 mins   cook time 25 mins

   per muffin

Preheat the oven to 180°C, fan 160°C, gas mark 4, and mist 8 x WW 2 in 1 Mini Cake Moulds with **calorie controlled cooking spray**. In a bowl, combine 180g **plain flour**, 2 teaspoons **baking powder**, ¼ teaspoon **bicarbonate of soda** and ¼ teaspoon **salt**. In a jug, whisk 60ml **skimmed milk** with 100ml **agave syrup**, 1 **egg**, 1 teaspoon **vanilla extract** and 60g **low-fat spread**, melted and cooled, until combined. Add the wet ingredients to the dry ingredients; stir until smooth. Fold in 100g diced **rhubarb** and the grated zest of 1 **orange**. Divide half the batter between the cake moulds. Measure out 125g **ready-to-serve low-fat custard**, then put 1 teaspoon of the custard into each mould. Spoon over the remaining batter, scatter over 50g diced rhubarb and top with the remaining custard. Bake for 20-25 minutes.

TO STORE Keep the muffins in an airtight container for up to 2 days, or wrap and freeze individually for up to 1 month. Defrost at room temperature.

Cook the week

100 **Introduction**

102 **Cook the week: family plan**

105 **Chorizo-crusted cod with roasted cauliflower & potatoes**

106 **Beef kofta flatbreads**

107 **Spaghetti with chorizo crumb**

108 **Slow-roasted cherry tomato pizza**

109 **Meat-feast pasta bake**

110 **Cook the week: for 2 plan**

113 **Kebab-shop houmous with sumac chicken & onion salad**

114 **Prawn burgers with edamame pods**

115 **Harissa vegetable gyros**

116 **Steak with cauliflower & horseradish purée**

117 **Seafood pies**

118 **Cook the week: veggie plan**

121 **Smoky tofu chilli with quinoa**

122 **Teriyaki mushroom meatballs with edamame soba noodles**

123 **Quinoa & halloumi stuffed peppers**

124 **Spiced root vegetable & lentil soup with breadsticks**

125 **Smoky tofu chilli pie with cornbread topping**

A new approach to
batch cooking

Get five days of tasty, homemade dinners ready in just one afternoon with our clever Cook the Week meal plans. Whether you're following a meat-free diet, cooking for two people or feeding a family, we have a plan that's perfect for you.

The premise is simple: get ahead of the midweek meal game by using a few hours at the weekend to plan what you're eating for dinner that week and get most of your prep out of the way. By Sunday evening you'll be kicking back, enjoying a sense of calm about the week ahead, and looking forward to five delicious stay-on-track weeknight meals.

Our three Cook The Week plans provide you with step-by-step guides to preparing creative evening meals in one go. They'll save you time and money, reduce the stress of planning and prepping a different meal each evening, help you to stay on track, and give you time to relax. Sounds good, right? Here's how to get started...

Shop for ingredients

You'll need all your ingredients at the start of your cooking session, so shop for groceries in advance, using the shopping lists provided. We've assumed you already have storecupboard ingredients – such as calorie controlled cooking spray, spices and flour – and have listed these, far right. So double check your cupboards before doing your shop. Buying only the ingredients you'll need avoids food waste and helps keep costs down.

Prep your kitchen

Before you get started, read through the step-by-step guide for the plan of your choice, so you have a clear idea of what you'll need to do when.

Then, set out your ingredients on a kitchen counter or tabletop. It's a good idea to have kitchen equipment at the ready, and in easy reach. For each of the plans you'll need the usual assortment of pots, pans, baking dishes and utensils, but you'll also need storage. All the food you prep and make during your cooking session will need to be sealed and stored correctly in the fridge or freezer, so check you have enough airtight containers, food bags or wraps to do the job.

Start cooking

Each of the step-by-step guides walks you through the entire cook-up session for the plan you've chosen. Unlike a regular recipe, you'll be cooking more than one meal at once, or prepping one element while cooking another. But don't be daunted! The methods are simple and designed with home cooks in mind. The process will take a few hours, but feel free to break it up into shorter sessions across the day, or lose yourself in some music or a podcast, get prepping and enjoy the process.

Tuck into the results

At the end of your cooking session, you'll have created the foundations for five meals. You'll still need to do some prep each day before dinner is on the table (don't worry, though, it takes little effort as the hard work is already out of the way). Happy cooking!

FROM YOUR STORECUPBOARD

ALL PLANS
Salt and pepper
Calorie controlled cooking spray
Self-raising flour
Smoked paprika
Ground cumin
Cumin seeds

FAMILY PLAN (P.102)
Rapeseed oil
Red wine vinegar
Balsamic vinegar
Coriander seeds
Ground coriander
Fennel seeds
Ground cinnamon
Chilli flakes
Dried oregano
Tomato purée
Agave syrup
Light brown soft sugar

FOR 2 PLAN (P.110)
Olive oil
Sesame oil
Soy sauce
Sriracha sauce
Pomegranate molasses
Sumac
Chilli flakes
Dried mint (optional)
Plain flour

VEGGIE PLAN (P.118)
Plain flour
Porridge oats
Baking powder
Dried oregano
Garam masala
Ground cinnamon
Hot chilli powder
Tomato purée
Vegetable stock cubes

Cook the week: family

There'll be no more cries of 'What's for dinner?' with this family-friendly feast of pasta, pizza, koftas and more.

Monday

Tuesday

Wednesday

Thursday

Friday

Your step-by-step cook-up guide

STEP 1

Start by making the **Slow-roasted Tomatoes**. Preheat the oven to 140°C, fan 120°C, gas mark 1. Put 500g **vine cherry tomatoes** in a roasting tin with 2 sliced **garlic** cloves and 2 sprigs **fresh rosemary**. Add ½ tablespoon **light brown soft sugar** and 1 teaspoon **salt**, then drizzle over 1 tablespoon each **rapeseed oil** and **red wine vinegar**. Put in the oven to roast (they'll take 1 hour).

STEP 2

Once they're in the oven, make a start on the **Rich Tomato Sauce**. Mist a large pan with **calorie controlled cooking spray** and set over a low heat. Finely dice 2 **onions** and add to the pan, then fry for 6-8 minutes, until soft.

STEP 3

While they're softening, prep the spices for the **Pickled Onions**. Put 1 teaspoon each **coriander** and **cumin seeds** in a frying pan and toast over a medium heat for 1-2 minutes. Transfer to a pestle and mortar and lightly crush.

STEP 4

Check on the onions for the Rich Tomato Sauce: give them a stir. Finely slice 3 **garlic** cloves, add these to the onions in the pan and cook, stirring, for 1 minute. Stir in 2 tablespoons **tomato purée** and cook for 2 minutes, then add 4 x 400g tins **chopped tomatoes**, 6 sprigs **fresh thyme**, 2 tablespoons **balsamic vinegar** and 1 tablespoon

agave syrup. Half fill one of the tomato tins with water and use this to swill out each tin into the pan. Give it all a good stir and bring to the boil. Meanwhile, cut out a circle of greaseproof paper that's the same size as the pan. Reduce the heat to a low simmer, and put the circle of paper over the sauce – this creates a lid, but allows steam to escape. Simmer until you have a thick, rich sauce – this will take about 1 hour.

STEP 5

While your sauce is simmering, turn back to the Pickled Onions. Put the crushed spices into a pan with 100ml **cider vinegar**, 1 tablespoon **agave syrup** and 1 teaspoon **salt**. Slice 3 **red onions** and add these to the pan. Give it all a stir and heat over a low heat for 2-3 minutes, then remove from the heat and set aside to cool to room temperature before sealing in a clean sterilised jar and storing in the fridge.

STEP 6

Check your Slow-roasted Tomatoes: they should be starting to soften now, but won't yet have started caramelising so will need a little longer. You can now prep your **Chorizo Crumb**. Slice 125g **chorizo** and 2 **garlic** cloves and set aside. Heat a dry frying pan over a medium heat and add the chorizo. Fry for 3-4 minutes, or until the chorizo releases oil and starts to crisp up. Add the garlic and cook for 1 minute, then remove from the heat and let cool

SHOPPING LIST

FRESH FRUIT, VEG & HERBS
500g baby new potatoes
1 medium cauliflower
3 red onions
2 onions, finely diced
Garlic (10 cloves)
500g vine cherry tomatoes
1 red pepper
1 yellow pepper
2 x 200g bags mixed salad leaves
2 x 150g bags young leaf spinach
Fresh herbs (rosemary, thyme and flat-leaf parsley)
3 lemons

MEAT, FISH & POULTRY
500g extra lean (5% fat) beef mince
2 x 165g skinless chicken breast fillets
4 x 120g skinless cod fillets
125g chorizo
100g lean bacon medallions
100g pepperoni slices

EGGS & DAIRY
650g 0% fat natural Greek yogurt
125g light mozzarella
100g light feta

OTHER
4 x 400g tins chopped tomatoes
240g wholewheat penne pasta
240g wholewheat spaghetti
Ciabatta bread (you'll need 100g)
Apple cider vinegar (you'll need 100ml)

slightly. While it's cooling, tear 100g **ciabatta** into chunks and add to a food processor. Grate the zest of 1 **lemon** and pick 1 tablespoon **fresh thyme** leaves: add both to the food processor along with the chorizo and garlic. Blitz to a crumb then put in a bowl and season. Divide into 2 equal portions; set aside to cool completely.

STEP 7

Take another look at the Rich Tomato Sauce. It should be thickening up, but will need longer to reach the right consistency. From now on, stir it occasionally to prevent it catching.

STEP 8

While the Rich Tomato Sauce simmers away and the Slow-roasted Tomatoes near the end of their roasting time, prepare the **Beef Koftas**. Put 500g **extra-lean beef mince (5% fat)** into a bowl. Crush 2 **garlic** cloves and finely grate the zest of 1 **lemon**, then add these to the bowl with 1 teaspoon **ground cumin**, 2 teaspoons **ground coriander**, 1 teaspoon **smoked paprika** and ½ teaspoon **ground cinnamon**. Chop a handful of **fresh flat-leaf parsley** and add to the bowl, then season and mix together. Shape into 12 koftas, put onto a plate, cover and put in the fridge.

STEP 9

Your Slow-roasted Tomatoes should now be ready. Remove them from the oven and set aside to cool completely before sealing in an airtight container and storing in the fridge.

STEP 10

Now, start the **Roasted Cauliflower and Potatoes**. Increase the oven temperature to 200°C, fan 180°C, gas mark 6. Put 500g **baby new potatoes** into a roasting tin, cutting any larger ones in half. Trim and cut 1 medium **cauliflower** into florets and add these to the tin. Drizzle over 1 tablespoon **rapeseed oil** and scatter over 1 teaspoon **fennel seeds**. Season and roast in the oven until tender – 25-30 minutes.

STEP 11

By now, the Chorizo Crumb should be completely cool so you can prep your **Chorizo-crusted Cod**. Store one portion of the crumb in an airtight container in the fridge. Line a large airtight container with baking paper and put 4 x 120g **skinless cod fillets** inside. Press the remaining crumb onto the fish to form a crust, then seal and store in the fridge until needed.

STEP 12

Give your Rich Tomato Sauce a final stir, then remove it from the heat. It's now time to make the **Meat-feast Pasta Bake**. Fill a large pan with water, add a pinch of salt and bring to the boil. While the water is coming to the boil, cut 2 x 165g **skinless chicken breast fillets** into thin strips and slice 100g **lean bacon medallions**. Deseed 1 **red** and 1 **yellow pepper** then slice each and set aside.

STEP 13

The water should be boiling now, so add 240g **wholewheat penne** to the pan, bring back to the boil and cook until just tender – this will take 10-12 minutes. Take a look at the Roasted Cauliflower and Potatoes – they should be ready now, so remove from the oven and set aside to cool completely before storing in an airtight container in the fridge.

STEP 14

Now, back to your Meat-feast Pasta Bake. Mist a large nonstick frying pan with cooking spray and fry the chicken and bacon for 2-3 minutes. Add the peppers along with ½ teaspoon **chilli flakes** and 1 teaspoon **dried oregano**, and continue to cook for 6-8 minutes, or until the peppers are softened.

STEP 15

While the pasta is boiling and the veg is softening, portion out your Rich Tomato Sauce. Take 2 airtight containers and put 500g of the sauce in 1 and 250g of sauce into the other. Seal and store in the fridge. Add the

remaining 750g tomato sauce to the pan of chicken, bacon and peppers, and stir well. Add 100g **pepperoni slices**, stir again, then remove from the heat. By now the pasta should be ready, so drain well, reserving half a cup of the pasta cooking water. Stir the pasta through the tomato sauce, adding some of the reserved pasta water until you get a nice coating consistency. Season to taste, then transfer to a large baking dish and set aside to cool completely.

STEP 16

While the Meat-feast Pasta Bake and Roasted Cauliflower and Potatoes are cooling, make the **Flatbreads**. Put 250g **self-raising flour** into a bowl. Season then add 250g **0% fat natural Greek yogurt** and stir until a dough forms. Dust a surface with 10g flour, then tip the dough out onto it. Knead for 2 minutes until smooth, then divide it into 8 balls. Roll out each ball to a circle and transfer to a piece of baking paper, dusted with a little of the flour to ensure they don't stick. Stack them and put in a freezer bag, then freeze until required.

STEP 17

Finally, make a **Lemon Yogurt Dressing**. Put 400g **0% fat natural Greek yogurt** into a bowl. Add 1 crushed **garlic** clove along with the zest and juice 1 **lemon** and a handful of chopped **fresh flat-leaf parsley**. Whisk together then season to taste. Divide into 2 equal portions and store in airtight containers in the fridge.

STEP 18

Your work is nearly done! Everything you need for the week is stored and in the fridge or freezer. The last thing to do is to slice 125g **light mozzarella** and layer the slices on the top of the cooled Meat-feast Pasta Bake. Wrap the bake in clingfilm then foil and freeze until Thursday night, when you'll remove from the freezer and allow to defrost overnight ahead of baking on Friday.

MONDAY
Chorizo-crusted cod with roasted cauliflower & potatoes

serves 4   **prep time 5 minutes**   **cook time 20 minutes**

(**8**) (**7**) (**4**) per serving

Preheat the oven to 200°C, fan 180°C, gas mark 6. Remove the **chorizo-crusted cod, roasted cauliflower and potatoes**, and 1 x quantity of **lemon yogurt dressing** from the fridge. Line a baking tray with baking paper, then transfer the fish to the tray and put it onto the top shelf of the oven. Tip the roasted vegetables into a roasting tin, and put it onto the bottom shelf of the oven. Bake for 18-20 minutes, until the fish is cooked through with a crisp and golden crumb, and the vegetables are piping hot. Stir 200g **young leaf spinach** through the vegetables to wilt, then serve with the fish and the lemon yogurt dressing.

TUESDAY
Beef kofta flatbreads
serves 4 **prep time 5 minutes** **cook time 10 minutes**

9 **8** **8** per serving

Remove the **beef koftas** from the fridge around 30 minutes before you want to cook them. Heat 1 tablespoon **rapeseed oil** in a large frying pan and fry the koftas for 6-8 minutes, turning regularly, until browned all over and cooked through. Meanwhile, remove 4 **flatbreads** from the freezer and defrost – this will take about 5-10 minutes. Heat another nonstick frying pan or griddle pan over a medium-high heat and cook the flatbreads for 45 seconds on one side, then turn and cook for 20-30 seconds on the other side. Remove from the pan and set aside in a clean, folded tea towel while you cook the remaining flatbreads. Remove the **pickled onions** and remaining portion of **lemon yogurt dressing** from the fridge. Top the flatbreads with a handful of **salad leaves**, three koftas, some of the pickled onions and the yogurt dressing.

WEDNESDAY
Spaghetti with chorizo crumb
serves 4   prep time 5 minutes   cook time 15 minutes

9   9   4   per serving

Preheat the oven to 200°C, fan 180°C, gas mark 6 and remove the **chorizo crumb** from the fridge. Cook 240g **wholewheat spaghetti** in a pan of boiling water to pack instructions, then drain and set aside, reserving half a cup of the pasta cooking water. Meanwhile, put the chorizo crumb on a baking tray and heat in the oven for 6-8 minutes, or until crisp; tip 1 x 500g portion **rich tomato sauce** into a pan and heat until simmering. Toss the cooked spaghetti with the tomato sauce, adding a little of the reserved pasta water for a thinner sauce. Divide the pasta between bowls and scatter over the chorizo crumb and some **fresh thyme** leaves, to serve.

THURSDAY
Slow-roasted cherry tomato pizza
serves 4   **prep time 5 minutes**   **cook time 15 minutes**

7 **7** **7** per serving

Preheat the oven to 200°C, gas 180°C, gas mark 6.
Meanwhile, remove 4 **flatbreads** from the freezer and
transfer to a large baking tray. Wilt 100g **young leaf
spinach** in the microwave for 2 minutes. Spread 1 x 250g
portion **rich tomato sauce** over the flatbreads, then
top with the wilted spinach and the **slow-roasted cherry
tomatoes**. Scatter over 100g **light feta** and bake for
10-12 minutes, until the pizza base is crisp.

FRIDAY
Meat-feast pasta bake
serves 4   **prep time 5 minutes**   **cook time 35 minutes**

13   **13**   **7**   per serving

Remove the defrosted **meat-feast pasta bake** from the fridge. Preheat the oven to 200°C, fan 180°C, gas mark 6. Bake the pasta bake for 35-40 minutes or until the sauce is bubbling and piping hot throughout and the cheese is melted and golden. Serve the pasta bake with 200g **mixed salad leaves** on the side.

Cook the week: for 2

Fitness sessions, social events, boxset marathons... with dinner already sorted, you'll have more time together to do the things you love.

Monday

Tuesday

Wednesday

Thursday

Friday

Your step-by-step cook-up guide

STEP 1

Start by roasting the **Harissa Vegetables** for Wednesday's gyros. Preheat the oven to 200°C, fan 180°C, gas mark 6. Trim 150g **baby carrots** and put them into a bowl. Trim 1 **fennel** bulb and 1 small **aubergine**, then cut each into wedges and add to the carrots in the bowl. Add 1 tablespoon **harissa paste**, 1 teaspoon **olive oil** and ½ teaspoon **cumin seeds**. Toss everything together, then season and transfer to a roasting tin. Put in the oven to roast (they'll take about 15-20 minutes).

STEP 2

Once they're in the oven, start the **Cauliflower and Potato Mash**. Cut 1 large **cauliflower** into florets (you'll need 500g) and put into a pan. Peel and chop 250g (prepared weight) **potatoes** and add to the pan. Cover with water, add a pinch of salt and bring to the boil. Reduce the heat and simmer for 15 minutes, until tender.

STEP 3

While your vegetables are roasting and simmering, make a start on the **Seafood Pie** filling. To make a white sauce, melt 15g **low-fat spread** in a small pan set over a medium heat. Whisk in 15g **plain flour** to form a paste, and cook for 1-2 minutes. Gradually add 350ml **semi-skimmed milk** to the pan, whisking as you go, until the mixture is smooth and combined. Season well and cook

over a low heat for 6-8 minutes, until the sauce is smooth and thickened.

STEP 4

While the white sauce is simmering, check on your Harissa Vegetables – if they're ready, remove from the oven and set aside to cool completely. If not, leave them to cook a little longer, but don't forget about them!

STEP 5

Turn your attention back to the filling for the seafood pie: devein 80g raw and peeled **king prawns** and set aside. Drain 60g **artichokes in brine** and 1 tablespoon **capers**, then pat both dry and roughly chop. Next, chop 1 tablespoon each **fresh flat-leaf parsley** and **chives**. Set everything aside. The white sauce should be ready, so remove it from the heat and let cool.

STEP 6

Check back in on your Cauliflower and Potato Mash. The veg should be tender to the touch by now, so drain and then return to the pan and mash with 30ml **semi-skimmed milk** and 20g **low-fat spread**. Season to taste and divide into 2 equal portions. Add 2 tablespoons chopped **fresh chives** to one portion, then set this aside to use as a topping for the Seafood Pie. Put the second portion into a mini food processor with 2 teaspoons **horseradish sauce**. Blitz so you have a **Cauliflower & Horseradish Purée**.

SHOPPING LIST

FRESH FRUIT, VEG & HERBS
1 large cauliflower
250g potatoes
150g baby carrots
1 fennel bulb
1 small aubergine
100g asparagus
120g watercress
Bag mixed radishes
1 iceberg lettuce
½ cucumber
4 plum tomatoes
Spring onions
3 onions
1 small green chilli
Garlic (3 cloves)
Ginger (small knob)
Fresh herbs (flat-leaf parsley, coriander and chives)
3 lemons

MEAT, FISH & POULTRY
2 x 225g sirloin steaks
2 x 165g packs raw king prawns
2 x 165g skinless chicken breasts
320g pack fresh fish pie mix
(we used Sainsbury's)

EGGS & DAIRY
380ml semi-skimmed milk
200g 0% fat natural Greek yogurt
Parmesan (you'll need 15g)
Light feta (you'll need 20g)
Low-fat spread

CHILLED & FROZEN
200g frozen edamame pods

OTHER
2 x 50g brioche burger buns
Lighter Than Light Mayonnaise
Harissa paste
2 x 400g tins chickpeas
Artichokes in brine
Tahini
Capers
Horseradish sauce

Transfer the purée into an airtight container and let cool completely before sealing and storing in the fridge until ready to serve with the griddled steak on Thursday.

STEP 7

Now you can make a marinade for the **Sumac Chicken**. Put 2 x 165g **skinless chicken breast fillets** into a plastic food bag and bash with a rolling pin to flatten slightly. Add 40g **0% fat natural Greek yogurt**, 1 small crushed **garlic** clove, the zest of 1 **lemon**, 1 teaspoon **sumac**, ½ teaspoon **paprika** and ½ teaspoon **ground cumin** to the bag. Use your hands to crush 2 ripe **plum tomatoes** into the bag so that they break up. Seal the bag, massage it all together, then store in the fridge.

STEP 8

Now you can finish assembling the Seafood Pies. Stir a 320g pack **fish pie mix** into the white sauce along with the prepared prawns, artichokes, capers and herbs. Season well then tip the mixture into 2 x 20cm pie dishes. Spoon over the cauliflower and chive mash and drag a fork across the surface to create a pattern. Grate 15g **Parmesan** and scatter over the top of the mash. Set aside to cool completely.

STEP 9

Now, make the **Harissa Flatbreads**. Put 80g **self-raising flour** into a bowl and season well. In a small bowl, stir 1 teaspoon **harissa paste** into 80g **0% fat natural Greek yogurt**, then add to the flour and mix until a soft dough forms. Dust a surface with 10g flour and knead the dough until smooth. Divide into 2 pieces and roll out each one to a thin 22cm circle. Layer the flatbreads between baking paper, wrap in clingfilm and freeze until required.

'Everything you need for the week ahead is stored in the fridge or freezer until needed'

STEP 10

Once the flatbreads are in the freezer, move onto the **Griddled Onions**. Heat a nonstick griddle pan to medium. Cut 3 medium **onions** into thick wedges and toss with 1 teaspoon **olive oil** and ½ teaspoon **sumac**. Thread the onions onto skewers and griddle, turning, for 20 minutes, until tender and charred.

STEP 11

While the onions are cooking, prepare the **Prawn Burgers**. Devein 250g raw and peeled **king prawns**, put 160g of them into a food processor, and reserve the rest. Deseed and chop 1 small **green chilli** and add to the processor with 2 tablespoons chopped **fresh coriander**. Season with pepper and blitz until the mixture comes together to a chunky paste – be careful not to overprocess or it will be mushy.

STEP 12

Keep checking on the Griddled Onions as they'll need to be turned regularly to prevent burning. Now, back to the Prawn Burgers. Put the prawn mixture in a bowl, then add 2 large grated **radishes** and 2 chopped **spring onions**. Cut each of the reserved prawns into 3-4 pieces, and fold these into the mixture. Shape the mixture into 2 burger patties, then layer between baking paper, put into a food bag and store in the fridge.

STEP 13

The Griddled Onions should be ready now. Remove from the skewers and let cool completely before sealing and storing in the fridge.

STEP 14

Next, you can make the **Oil-free Houmous** and **Garlic Yogurt Sauce**. First, drain 2 x 400g tins **chickpeas**, reserving the liquid from the tin. Store 120g chickpeas in an airtight container in the fridge – you'll need to use these later in the week. Put the remaining 360g chickpeas into a food processor with 1 small grated **garlic** clove, the juice of ½ **lemon** and 20g **tahini**. Add a good splash of the reserved chickpea water and blitz until creamy. Season to taste, adding more lemon juice if needed. If the houmous is too thick or grainy, keep adding a splash more chickpea water until it's creamy and fluffy. Divide the houmous into 2 equal portions and store in separate airtight containers in the fridge until needed.

STEP 15

For the Garlic Yogurt Sauce, combine 1 small crushed garlic clove with 80g **0% fat natural Greek yogurt**, the juice of ½ **lemon** and ¼ teaspoon **dried mint** (or ½ teaspoon chopped fresh mint). Season then divide into 2 equal portions and store in the fridge.

STEP 16

Your work is nearly done! Everything you need for the week is stored and in the fridge or freezer. The last thing to do is to wrap the cooled Seafood Pies in clingfilm then foil and freeze until Thursday night, when you'll remove them from the freezer and allow to defrost overnight in the fridge ahead of reheating on Friday.

MONDAY
Kebab-shop houmous with sumac chicken & onion salad

serves 2   **prep time 5 minutes**   **cook time 15 minutes**

7 **3** **3** per serving

Remove 1 x quantity **oil-free houmous**, the **griddled onions** and 1 x quantity **garlic yogurt sauce** from the fridge. Preheat the oven to 200°C, fan 180°C, gas mark 6. Put the onions on a baking tray and reheat in the oven for 10-15 minutes. Transfer to a bowl, drizzle over 1 tablespoon **pomegranate molasses** and sprinkle over ¼ teaspoon **sumac**. Season and top with a handful of **fresh flat-leaf parsley**. Meanwhile, mist a large griddle or frying pan with **calorie controlled cooking spray** and heat over a medium-high heat. Lift the **sumac chicken** from its marinade, shaking off any excess, then griddle for 15 minutes, turning, until cooked through. Remove from the pan and let rest for a few minutes before thickly slicing. Spread the houmous onto 2 plates, top with the chicken, a handful of shredded **iceberg lettuce** and some sliced **cucumber** and **plum tomatoes**. Drizzle over the garlic yogurt sauce and serve with the onion salad and **lemon wedges** on the side.

TUESDAY
Prawn burgers with edamame pods

serves 2

prep time 5 minutes   cook time 10 minutes

(12) (7) (7) per serving

Remove the **prawn patties** from the fridge.
To prepare the edamame, blanch 200g
frozen edamame pods in a pan of boiling
water for 2 minutes, then drain. In a bowl,
combine 1 teaspoon **soy sauce**, ½ teaspoon
sesame oil, ½ teaspoon grated **garlic** and
¼ teaspoon **chilli flakes**. Mist a nonstick
frying pan with **calorie controlled cooking
spray** and fry the edamame over a high
heat for 1-2 minutes until the pods start to
blister. Add the soy mixture and cook for
1-2 minutes, then remove from the heat and
scatter with **sea salt**. Meanwhile, mist
another frying pan with cooking spray
and cook the burgers over a medium heat
for 6 minutes, turning once. Combine
2 tablespoons Hellmann's **Lighter Than
Light Mayonnaise** with 2 teaspoons
sriracha sauce, and toast 2 x 50g **brioche
buns**. Fill the buns with **iceberg lettuce**
leaves, the prawn patties, sriracha mayo
and sliced **radishes**. Serve with the
edamame pods.

WEDNESDAY
Harissa vegetable gyros

serves 2   **prep time 5 minutes**   **cook time 20 minutes**

(13) (8) (8) per serving

Preheat the oven to 200°C, fan 180°C, gas mark 6. Remove the **flatbreads** from the freezer to defrost – this will take 5-10 minutes. Remove the **harissa veg**, remaining **oil-free houmous**, remaining **garlic yogurt sauce** and 120g **chickpeas** from the fridge. Put the chickpeas in a bowl, mist all over with **calorie controlled cooking spray**, then sprinkle over ½ teaspoon **sumac** and ¼ teaspoon **ground cumin**. Season, then toss to coat. Put on a baking tray with the harissa veg, then mist with cooking spray and warm in the oven for 20 minutes. Heat a dry frying pan over a high heat and cook the flatbreads, one at a time, for 1-2 minutes on each side. Spread the houmous over the flatbreads then top with the harissa veg and chickpeas, 20g **light feta**, 40g **watercress** and the garlic sauce.

THURSDAY
Steak with cauliflower & horseradish purée

serves 2   **prep time 5 minutes**   **cook time 10 minutes**

8   **8**   **7**   per serving

Remove the **cauliflower and horseradish purée** from the fridge. Heat a large nonstick griddle or frying pan over a high heat until very hot. Mist 2 x 225g **sirloin steaks** with **calorie controlled cooking spray** and season well. Griddle the steaks for 2 minutes on each side, or until cooked to your liking. Remove to a plate to rest for 10 minutes. While the steak is resting, warm the purée in a small pan over a low heat, or in the microwave. Divide the purée between plates, top with the steak, drizzle with the steak resting juices and serve with 40g **watercress**.

FRIDAY
Seafood pies
serves 2
prep time 5 minutes   cook time 30 minutes

(14) (8) (7) per serving

Remove the defrosted **seafood pies** from the fridge. Preheat the oven to 180°C, fan 160°C, gas mark 4. Put the pies on a baking tray and cook for 30 minutes, until the filling is bubbling and the mash is golden. Remove from the oven and let cool slightly. Cook 100g **asparagus** in a pan of boiling water for 1-2 minutes, then drain and refresh under cold water. Toss with 40g **watercress** and divide between plates. Squeeze over some **lemon juice** and serve with the pies.

Cook the week: veggie

Add some exciting new vegetarian meals to your repertoire
with these five creative flavour-packed dishes.

Monday

Tuesday

Wednesday

Thursday

Friday

Your step-by-step cook-up guide

STEP 1
Start the **Mushroom Meatballs**. Mist a large nonstick frying pan with **calorie controlled cooking spray**. Finely chop 700g **white mushrooms** then fry them over a medium heat for 10-15 minutes until the water evaporates.

STEP 2
While the mushrooms are cooking, press the tofu for the **Smoky Tofu Chilli**. Drain and pat dry 2 x 396g packs **firm tofu**, then wrap in kitchen paper and put on a flat surface. Sit a chopping board on top and weigh it down with a heavy object. Set aside for 30 minutes.

STEP 3
Turn back to the mushrooms. Give them a stir then chop 1 **onion**, crush 3 **garlic** cloves and measure out 2 teaspoons grated **ginger**; set these aside. Give the mushrooms a stir. If they're ready, tip them into a bowl. If not, let them continue to cook.

STEP 4
Make a start on the veg for the Smoky Tofu Chilli. Finely dice 2 **onions**, 2 **celery** sticks and 3 deseeded **red peppers**. Mist a deep nonstick frying pan with **calorie controlled cooking spray** and fry the veg with 3 tablespoons water for 6-8 minutes, until softened.

STEP 5
If your mushrooms are still cooking, they should be ready now, so tip them

into a bowl and mist the frying pan with more cooking spray. Stir-fry the prepped onion, garlic and ginger for 2 minutes, then add to the bowl of mushrooms and set aside to cool for at least 15 minutes.

STEP 6
Now, back to the Smoky Tofu Chilli. Once the veg has softened, slice 4 **garlic** cloves and add to the pan with 1 teaspoon **chilli powder**, 2 teaspoons **smoked paprika**, 2 teaspoons **ground cumin** and 1 teaspoon **dried oregano**. Cook, stirring, for 2 minutes, while you make up 500ml **vegetable stock** using water from the kettle and 1 stock cube. Add to the pan with 1 tablespoon **tomato purée** and 2 x 400g tins **chopped tomatoes**. Season and bring to the boil.

STEP 7
While the Smoky Tofu Chilli is coming to the boil, return to the Mushroom Meatballs. Add 150g fresh **wholemeal breadcrumbs**, 60g **porridge oats** and 3 tablespoons chopped **fresh coriander** to the mushroom mixture. Season and stir to combine, then add 2 beaten **eggs** and stir again. Chill in the fridge for 2 hours.

STEP 8
Next, unwrap the tofu and cut into 1.5cm cubes. Put in a bowl, add ½ teaspoon **hot chilli powder** and toss to coat. Mist a large nonstick frying pan with cooking spray and fry the tofu, in batches, over a high heat for 8-10 minutes. Keep an eye

SHOPPING LIST

FRESH FRUIT, VEG & HERBS
700g white mushrooms
300g carrots
300g sweet potatoes
200g parsnips
4 onions
9 spring onions
7 red peppers
2 celery sticks
80g mixed salad leaves
Fresh herbs (flat-leaf parsley and coriander)
Garlic (9 cloves)
Ginger (small knob)
1 green chilli
2 limes
2 lemons

EGGS & DAIRY
4 eggs
100ml semi-skimmed milk
500g 0% fat natural Greek yogurt
Reduced-fat soured cream (you'll need 80g)
WW Reduced Fat Grated Mature Cheese (you'll need 75g)
125g light halloumi
Low-fat spread

CHILLED & FROZEN
2 x 396g packs firm tofu
100g frozen edamame pods

OTHER
100g polenta
100g red lentils
400g tricolour quinoa
2 x 400g tins chopped tomatoes
2 x 400g tins black beans
200g 100% buckwheat soba noodles
100ml thick teriyaki sauce
Sundried tomatoes in oil (you'll need 40g)
Pitted kalamata olives in brine (you'll need 50g)
Fresh wholemeal breadcrumbs (you'll need 150g)

on the Smoky Tofu Chilli: it should be boiling now, so reduce the heat, cover and simmer for 45 minutes. Transfer the cooked tofu to a plate.

STEP 9
You can now prep the **Quinoa**. Rinse 400g **tricolour quinoa** then drain and tip into a large, deep nonstick frying pan. Stir over a medium heat to dry out. Once all the liquid has evaporated, mist with cooking spray and cook until the quinoa starts to pop – about 10 minutes. Make up 900ml **vegetable stock** using water from the kettle and 1 stock cube, then add to the pan and simmer for 20 minutes or until the stock is absorbed.

STEP 10
Check in on the Smoky Tofu Chilli: it should be thickening up now, so give it a good stir. Now, make the **Roasted Red Pepper** shells and **Breadsticks**.

STEP 11
Preheat the oven to 200°C, fan 180°C, gas mark 6 and line a baking tray with baking paper. In a bowl, combine 170g **self-raising flour**, 170g **0% fat natural Greek yogurt** and ½ teaspoon **salt** to make a dough. Divide the dough into 8 pieces. Dust a surface with 10g flour and roll each piece out to a 25cm-long breadstick. Put onto the tray and bake for 15-20 minutes. Meanwhile, cut 4 **red peppers** in half through the stalks and deseed. Put on a baking sheet, mist with cooking spray and roast with the breadsticks – they'll take 20 minutes.

STEP 12
Look at your Smoky Tofu Chilli – by now, it should have been bubbling for 45 minutes. Drain and rinse 2 x 400g tins **black beans**, then add to the chilli. Cook, uncovered, for 15 minutes.

STEP 13
The Quinoa should be ready now so remove it from the heat. Weigh 600g of the cooked quinoa and set aside to cool completely. Drain 50g pitted **Kalamata olives in brine** and 40g **sundried tomatoes in oil**, and pat both dry with kitchen paper. Chop them and add these

to the remaining 400g cooked quinoa. Stir in 3 tablespoons chopped **fresh flat-leaf parsley**, the zest of 1 **lemon** and the juice of ½ **lemon** (reserve the other ½ lemon for the soup in Step 20). Season and set aside to cool. Put both quinoa portions into airtight containers and store in the fridge.

STEP 14
Check the Roasted Red Pepper shells and Breadsticks – they should be ready, so set aside to cool. Leave the oven on for the Smoky Tofu Chilli Pie in Step 17. Layer the peppers between baking paper in an airtight container and store in the fridge. Wrap the breadsticks in clingfilm and put in the freezer.

STEP 15
Turn back to the Smoky Tofu Chilli. Add the fried tofu to the pan, stir, and simmer for 10 minutes.

STEP 16
Next, prep the cornbread topping for the Smoky Tofu Chilli Pie. Melt 25g **low-fat spread** in the microwave and set aside. Deseed and chop 1 **green chilli**, and chop 6 **spring onions**. Put these in a bowl, add 100g **polenta**, 100g **plain flour**, 1½ teaspoons **baking powder** and ½ teaspoon **salt**, then mix together. In a jug, combine the melted spread with 2 **eggs**, 100ml **semi-skimmed milk**, 50g **0% fat natural Greek yogurt** and 75g **WW Reduced Fat Grated Mature Cheese**. Stir the wet ingredients into the dry until combined; set aside.

STEP 17
By now, your Smoky Tofu Chilli should be rich and thick. Season, then remove from the heat and divide into 2 portions. Spoon 1 portion into a container and set aside to cool completely. To make the Smoky Tofu Chilli Pie, tip the remaining portion into a medium baking dish and spoon over the cornbread topping mixture. Bake for 30-35 minutes, until the topping is puffed and golden. Let cool completely.

STEP 18
While the Smoky Tofu Chilli Pie is in the oven, make the **Spiced Root Veg Soup**. Mist a large nonstick pan with cooking spray and fry 1 diced **onion** with 2 tablespoons water for 6-8 minutes, until soft. While the onion is cooking, peel and chop 300g **sweet potatoes**, 200g **parsnips** and 150g **carrots**. Make up 1.2 litres of **vegetable stock** using 2 stock cubes and boiling water from the kettle. Once the onion is softened, add 2 crushed **garlic** cloves, 2 teaspoons grated **ginger**, 1 teaspoon **cumin seeds** and 2 teaspoons **garam masala** to the pan and cook, stirring, for 1-2 minutes. Add the chopped veg with 100g **red lentils** and the stock, then bring to the boil. Once boiling, reduce the heat, cover, and let simmer for 30 minutes.

STEP 19
While the Spiced Root Veg Soup is simmering, finish the Mushroom Meatballs. Remove the mixture from the fridge and line a baking tray with baking paper. Shape the mushroom mixture into 16 balls and put on the tray. Mist with cooking spray and bake next to the chilli pie for 20 minutes. Remove from the oven and let cool completely.

STEP 20
While the Smoky Tofu Chilli Pie and Mushroom Meatballs are in the oven, give the Spiced Root Veg Soup a stir every now and then. After it's been simmering for 30 minutes, use a stick blender to blitz until smooth, then stir in 2 tablespoons **lemon juice** and season to taste. Set aside to cool completely.

STEP 21
Your work is nearly done! Almost everything you need for the week is in the fridge or freezer. Once everything else has cooled, put the Mushroom Meatballs and Spiced Root Veg Soup in containers in the fridge. Wrap the cooled Smoky Tofu Chilli Pie in clingfilm then foil and freeze until Thursday night, when you'll remove it from the freezer and defrost overnight in the fridge ahead of reheating on Friday.

MONDAY
Smoky tofu chilli with quinoa

serves 4   **prep time 5 minutes**   **cook time 10 minutes**

9 **6** **0** per serving

Remove the **cooked plain quinoa** and the **smoky tofu chilli** from the fridge. Gently reheat both in two separate pans, adding a splash of water to each and stirring occasionally, until piping hot. Meanwhile, trim and thinly slice 3 **spring onions** and cut 1 **lime** into wedges. Divide the quinoa and chilli between plates, top each portion with 50g **0% fat natural Greek yogurt**. Scatter over the spring onions and serve with the lime wedges on the side.

TUESDAY
Teriyaki mushroom meatballs with edamame soba noodles

serves 4   prep time 5 minutes   cook time 20 minutes

14   **12**   **5**   per serving

Remove the **mushroom meatballs** from the fridge. Mist a large nonstick frying pan with **calorie controlled cooking spray** and reheat the meatballs, over a medium heat, covered and turning occasionally, for 10 minutes. In a bowl, combine 100ml **thick teriyaki sauce** (we used Sainsbury's) with 100ml water, then pour this mixture over the meatballs. Continue to cook, stirring, for 5-7 minutes until the sauce has reduced and the meatballs are coated and sticky. Meanwhile, bring a pan of water to the boil then add 100g **frozen edamame beans**. Bring back to the boil, add 200g **100% buckwheat soba noodles** and cook for 3-4 minutes until both are tender. Drain, return to the pan, and toss with 150g **carrot**, cut into matchsticks, and the juice of 1 **lime**. Divide the noodles and meatballs between plates, and top with **fresh coriander**.

WEDNESDAY
Quinoa & halloumi stuffed peppers

serves 4 **prep time 10 minutes** **cook time 20 minutes**

8 **8** **4** per serving

Remove the **roasted red peppers** and **quinoa** from the fridge. Preheat the oven to 220°C, fan 200°C, gas mark 7. Put the peppers on a baking sheet and stuff with the quinoa. Top with 125g diced **light halloumi** and bake for 18-20 minutes until the halloumi is golden. Divide 80g **mixed salad leaves** between plates and serve with 2 halved peppers per person.

THURSDAY
Spiced root vegetable & lentil soup with breadsticks

serves 4   **prep time 5 minutes**   **cook time 10 minutes**

(12) (8) (5) per serving

Remove the **soup** from the fridge and the **breadsticks** from the freezer. Preheat the oven to 170°C, fan 150°C, gas mark 3½. Unwrap the breadsticks and put onto a baking tray. Warm in the oven for 8-10 minutes. Meanwhile, gently reheat the soup in a pan until piping hot. Ladle the soup into bowls and swirl 20g **0% fat natural Greek yogurt** into each portion. Scatter over a few **fresh coriander** leaves and serve with the breadsticks.

FRIDAY
Smoky tofu chilli pie with cornbread topping

serves 4 **prep time 10 minutes** **cook time 45 minutes**

12 **8** **8** per serving

Remove the defrosted **tofu chilli pie** from the fridge. Preheat the oven to 180°C, fan 160°C, gas mark 4. Put the pie on a baking tray and reheat, covered with foil, for 30 minutes. Uncover and continue to heat for a further 10-15 minutes until piping hot. Serve the pie topped with 1 tablespoon **reduced-fat soured cream** per person, and some sprigs of **fresh coriander**.

SmartPoints index

Green

0 SmartPoints
Chipotle butternut squash soup	40
'Creamy' mushroom soup	40

1 SmartPoint
Aubergine parmigiana bake	22
Pork polpette	58
Quinoa-crusted fish goujons	62

2 SmartPoints
Cod & butter bean fishcakes	36

3 SmartPoints
Carrot cake ice lollies	82
Chicken paprikash	28
Ginger & oat biscuits	80
Kale pesto	66
Rich Quorn ragù	54
Soy-poached chicken breast fillets	50
White bean & saffron soup	40

5 SmartPoints
Almond & cherry oat bars	88
Bircher muesli muffins	96
Braised cod with tomatoes, capers & olives	24
Chickpea tikka masala	38
Chinese pancakes with soy-poached chicken	51
Cheese & broccoli muffins	96
Cheese & Marmite English muffins	92
Scotch broth	40
Sweet potato & goat's cheese rösti	18

6 SmartPoints
Caramel cluster fro-yo	86
Frozen tiramisu slice	84
Greek yogurt cake	70
Goan fish curry	20
Indian-spiced Quorn ragù pot pies	55
Lemon & yogurt pancakes	90
Lentil & cauliflower dhal	46
Pear & blueberry crumbles	76
Rhubarb & custard muffins	96

7 SmartPoints
Beef & black bean stew	16
Beetroot & goat's cheese tarts	94
Cheesecake swirl brownies	78
Chicken chipolata & prawn jambalaya	32
Kebab-shop houmous with sumac chicken & onion salad	113
Lemon meringue pie cake	70
Mediterranean muffins	96
Slow-roasted cherry tomato pizza	108
Strawberry syrup cake	71

8 SmartPoints
Chicken & chestnut mushroom lasagne	30
Chorizo-crusted cod with roasted cauliflower & potatoes	105
Cinnamon & raisin swirl buns	74
Crispy fish tacos with lime slaw & mango salsa	62
Lamb shepherd's pie	34
Orange & pistachio cake	71
Quinoa & halloumi stuffed peppers	123
Quorn ragù tortilla bake	55
Steak with cauliflower & horseradish purée	116

9 SmartPoints
Beef kofta flatbreads	106
Fish goujons with crushed ricotta peas	63
Fusilli with kale pesto & tomatoes	66
Lentil spaghetti with Quorn ragù	54
Pork & leek pie	26
Pork polpette pittas with harissa yogurt	59
Smoky tofu chilli with quinoa	121
Spaghetti with chorizo crumb	107

10 SmartPoints
Dhal with mango chutney chicken	46
Pesto chicken cobbler	67
Sicilian pork polpette bake	59

11 SmartPoints
Chicken, mushroom & kale pesto pizza	67
Chinese soy-poached chicken noodle soup	51
Roti-style wraps with dhal	47
Soy-poached chicken with ginger fried rice	50
Sticky hoisin pork polpette with rice	58

12 SmartPoints
Prawn burgers with edamame pods	114
Smoky tofu chilli pie with cornbread topping	125
Spiced root vegetable & lentil soup with breadsticks	124

13 SmartPoints
Dhal traybake with spiced salmon	47
Fish goujons with Mexican-style rice	63
Meat-feast pasta bake	109
Harissa vegetable gyros	115

14 SmartPoints
Seafood pies	117
Teriyaki mushroom meatballs with edamame soba noodles	122

Blue

0 SmartPoints
Chipotle butternut squash soup	40
'Creamy' mushroom soup	40

1 SmartPoint
Aubergine parmigiana bake	22
Cod & butter bean fishcakes	36
Lentil & cauliflower dhal	46
Pork polpette	58
Quinoa-crusted fish goujons	62
Rich Quorn ragù	54

2 SmartPoints
Chicken paprikash	28
Chickpea tikka masala	38
Soy-poached chicken breast fillets	50
White bean & saffron soup	40

3 SmartPoints
Dhal with mango chutney chicken	46
Dhal traybake with spiced salmon	47
Indian-spiced Quorn ragù pot pies	55
Kale pesto	66
Ginger & oat biscuits	80
Carrot cake ice lollies	82
Kebab-shop houmous with sumac chicken & onion salad	113

4 SmartPoints
Cheese & broccoli muffins	96
Chinese pancakes with soy-poached chicken	51
Sweet potato & goat's cheese rösti	18

5 SmartPoints
Almond & cherry oat bars	88
Bircher muesli muffins	96
Braised cod with tomatoes, capers & olives	24
Caramel cluster fro-yo	86
Cheese & Marmite English muffins	92
Goan fish curry	20
Lemon & yogurt pancakes	90
Scotch broth	40

6 SmartPoints
Beef & black bean stew	16
Beetroot & goat's cheese tarts	94
Chicken chipolata & prawn jambalaya	32
Cheesecake swirl brownies	78
Fish goujons with crushed ricotta peas	63
Frozen tiramisu slice	84
Greek yogurt cake	70
Mediterranean muffins	96
Pear & blueberry crumbles	76
Quorn ragù tortilla bake	55
Rhubarb & custard muffins	96
Roti-style wraps with dhal	47
Smoky tofu chilli with quinoa	121

Purple

7 SmartPoints
Chicken & chestnut mushroom lasagne 30
Chorizo-crusted cod with roasted
  cauliflower & potatoes 105
Cinnamon & raisin swirl buns 74
Crispy fish tacos with lime slaw
  & mango salsa 62
Lentil spaghetti with Quorn ragù 54
Lemon meringue pie cake 70
Prawn burgers with edamame pods 114
Slow-roasted cherry tomato pizza 108
Strawberry syrup cake 71

8 SmartPoints
Beef kofta flatbreads 106
Chinese soy-poached chicken
  noodle soup 51
Harissa vegetable gyros 115
Lamb shepherd's pie 34
Orange & pistachio cake 71
Pesto chicken cobbler 67
Pork polpette pittas with harissa yogurt 59
Quinoa & halloumi stuffed peppers 123
Seafood pies 117
Smoky tofu chilli pie with
  cornbread topping 125
Spiced root vegetable & lentil
  soup with breadsticks 124
Steak with cauliflower
  & horseradish purée 116

9 SmartPoints
Fish goujons with Mexican-style rice 63
Fusilli with kale pesto & tomatoes 66
Pork & leek pie 26
Sicilian pork polpette bake 59
Soy-poached chicken with
  ginger fried rice 50
Spaghetti with chorizo crumb 107

10 SmartPoints
Chicken, mushroom & kale pesto pizza 67

11 SmartPoints
Sticky hoisin pork polpette with rice 58

12 SmartPoints
Teriyaki mushroom meatballs
  with edamame soba noodles 122

13 SmartPoints
Meat-feast pasta bake 109

0 SmartPoints
Chipotle butternut squash soup 40
'Creamy' mushroom soup 40
Smoky tofu chilli with quinoa 121

1 SmartPoint
Aubergine parmigiana bake 22
Cod & butter bean fishcakes 36
Indian-spiced Quorn ragù pot pies 55
Lentil & cauliflower dhal 46
Pork polpette 58
Quinoa-crusted fish goujons 62
Rich Quorn ragù 54

2 SmartPoints
Chicken paprikash 28
Chickpea tikka masala 38
Fish goujons with Mexican-style rice 63
Soy-poached chicken breast fillets 50
Sweet potato & goat's cheese rösti 18
White bean & saffron soup 40

3 SmartPoints
Carrot cake ice lollies 82
Dhal traybake with spiced salmon 47
Dhal with mango chutney chicken 46
Fusilli with kale pesto & tomatoes 66
Ginger & oat biscuits 80
Kale pesto 66
Kebab-shop houmous with sumac
  chicken & onion salad 113
Lentil spaghetti with Quorn ragù 54

4 SmartPoints
Almond & cherry oat bars 88
Bircher muesli muffins 96
Cheese & broccoli muffins 96
Chinese pancakes with
  soy-poached chicken 51
Chorizo-crusted cod with roasted
  cauliflower & potatoes 105
Quinoa & halloumi stuffed peppers 123
Spaghetti with chorizo crumb 107

5 SmartPoints
Braised cod with tomatoes,
  capers & olives 24
Caramel cluster fro-yo 86
Chicken & chestnut mushroom lasagne 30
Cheese & Marmite English muffins 92
Fish goujons with crushed ricotta peas 63
Goan fish curry 20
Lemon & yogurt pancakes 90
Pear & blueberry crumbles 76
Scotch broth 40
Spiced root vegetable & lentil
  soup with breadsticks 124
Teriyaki mushroom meatballs
  with edamame soba noodles 122

6 SmartPoints
Beef & black bean stew 16
Beetroot & goat's cheese tarts 94
Cheesecake swirl brownies 78
Chicken chipolata & prawn jambalaya 32
Crispy fish tacos with lime slaw
  & mango salsa 62
Frozen tiramisu slice 84
Greek yogurt cake 70
Mediterranean muffins 96
Quorn ragù tortilla bake 55
Rhubarb & custard muffins 96
Roti-style wraps with dhal 47

7 SmartPoints
Cinnamon & raisin swirl buns 74
Lemon meringue pie cake 70
Meat-feast pasta bake 109
Prawn burgers with edamame pods 114
Seafood pies 117
Slow-roasted cherry tomato pizza 108
Steak with cauliflower
  & horseradish purée 116
Strawberry syrup cake 71

8 SmartPoints
Beef kofta flatbreads 106
Chinese soy-poached chicken
  noodle soup 51
Harissa vegetable gyros 115
Lamb shepherd's pie 34
Orange & pistachio cake 71
Pesto chicken cobbler 67
Pork polpette pittas with harissa yogurt 59
Smoky tofu chilli pie with
  cornbread topping 125
Sticky hoisin pork polpette with rice 58

9 SmartPoints
Pork & leek pie 26
Sicilian pork polpette bake 59
Soy-poached chicken with
  ginger fried rice 50

10 SmartPoints
Chicken, mushroom & kale pesto pizza 67

Recipe index

Almond & cherry oat bars 88
AUBERGINES
Aubergine parmigiana bake 22
BACON
Meat-feast pasta bake 109
BEEF
Beef & black bean stew 16
Beef kofta flatbreads 106
Steak with cauliflower &
horseradish purée 116
Beef & black bean stew 16
Beef kofta flatbreads 106
BEETROOT
Beetroot & goat's cheese tarts 94
BERRIES
Bircher muesli muffins 96
Cheesecake swirl brownies 78
Pear & blueberry crumbles 76
Strawberry syrup cake 71
Bircher muesli muffins 96
Braised cod with tomatoes,
capers & olives 24
BREAD
Beef kofta flatbreads 106
Cheese & Marmite English muffins 92
Cinnamon & raisin swirl buns 74
Harissa vegetable gyros 115
Pork polpette pittas with harissa yogurt 59
Quorn ragù tortilla bake 55
Roti-style wraps with dhal 47
Harissa vegetable gyros 115
BROCCOLI
Cheese & broccoli muffins 96
BURGERS
Prawn burgers with edamame pods 114
BUTTERNUT SQUASH
Chipotle butternut squash soup 40
Lamb shepherd's pie 34

CABBAGE
Crispy fish tacos with lime
slaw & mango salsa 62
CAKES
Cheesecake swirl brownies 78
Greek yogurt cake 70
Lemon meringue pie cake 70
Orange & pistachio cake 71
Strawberry syrup cake 71
Caramel cluster fro-yo 86
Carrot cake ice lollies 82
CARROTS
Carrot cake ice lollies 82
Harissa vegetable gyros 115
Spiced root vegetable & lentil
soup with breadsticks 124
CAULIFLOWER
Chorizo-crusted cod with roasted
cauliflower & potatoes 105
Dhal traybake with spiced salmon 47
Dhal with mango chutney chicken 46

Lentil & cauliflower dhal 46
Roti-style wraps with dhal 47
Seafood pies 117
Steak with cauliflower &
horseradish purée 116
CHEESE
Aubergine parmigiana bake 22
Beetroot & goat's cheese tarts 94
Cheese & broccoli muffins 96
Cheese & Marmite English muffins 92
Chicken, mushroom & kale pesto pizza 67
Meat-feast pasta bake 109
Mediterranean muffins 96
Quinoa & halloumi stuffed peppers 123
Quorn ragù tortilla bake 55
Sicilian pork polpette bake 59
Slow-roasted cherry tomato pizza 108
Sweet potato & goat's cheese rösti 18
Cheese & broccoli muffins 96
Cheese & Marmite English muffins 92
Cheesecake swirl brownies 78
CHERRIES
Almond & cherry oat bars 88
CHICKEN
Chicken & chestnut mushroom lasagne 30
Chicken chipolata & prawn jambalaya 32
Chicken, mushroom & kale pesto pizza 67
Chicken paprikash 28
Chinese pancakes with
soy-poached chicken 51
Chinese soy-poached chicken
noodle soup 51
Dhal with mango chutney chicken 46
Kebab-shop houmous with
sumac chicken & onion salad 113
Meat-feast pasta bake 109
Pesto chicken cobbler 67
Soy-poached chicken breast fillets 50
Soy-poached chicken with
ginger fried rice 50
Chicken & chestnut mushroom lasagne 30
Chicken chipolata & prawn jambalaya 32
Chicken, mushroom & kale pesto pizza 67
Chicken paprikash 28
Chickpea tikka masala 38
CHICKPEAS
Chickpea tikka masala 38
Harissa vegetable gyros 115
Chinese pancakes with
soy-poached chicken 51
Chinese soy-poached chicken
noodle soup 51
Chipotle butternut squash soup 40
CHOCOLATE
Cheesecake swirl brownies 78
Frozen tiramisu slice 84
CHORIZO
Chorizo-crusted cod with roasted
cauliflower & potatoes 105
Spaghetti with chorizo crumb 107

Chorizo-crusted cod with roasted
cauliflower & potatoes 105
Cinnamon & raisin swirl buns 74
COCONUT
Goan fish curry 20
Cod & butter bean fishcakes 36
'Creamy' mushroom soup 40
Crispy fish tacos with lime
slaw & mango salsa 62
CURRY
Chickpea tikka masala 38
Dhal traybake with spiced salmon 47
Dhal with mango chutney chicken 46
Goan fish curry 20
Indian-spiced Quorn ragù pot pies 55
Lentil & cauliflower dhal 46
Roti-style wraps with dhal 47

Dhal traybake with spiced salmon 47
Dhal with mango chutney chicken 46

EDAMAME
Prawn burgers with edamame pods 114
Teriyaki mushroom meatballs with
edamame soba noodles 122
FISH
Braised cod with tomatoes,
capers & olives 24
Chorizo-crusted cod with roasted
cauliflower & potatoes 105
Cod & butter bean fishcakes 36
Crispy fish tacos with lime
slaw & mango salsa 62
Dhal traybake with spiced salmon 47
Fish goujons with crushed
ricotta peas 63
Fish goujons with Mexican-style rice 63
Goan fish curry 20
Quinoa-crusted fish goujons 62
Seafood pies 117
Fish goujons with crushed
ricotta peas 63
Fish goujons with Mexican-style rice 63
Frozen tiramisu slice 84
Fusilli with kale pesto & tomatoes 66

HOUMOUS
Harissa vegetable gyros 115
Kebab-shop houmous with
sumac chicken & onion salad 113

Ginger & oat biscuits 80
Goan fish curry 20
Greek yogurt cake 70

HARISSA
Harissa vegetable gyros 115
Pork polpette pittas with
harissa yogurt 59
Harissa vegetable gyros 115

HORSERADISH
Steak with cauliflower &
horseradish purée 116

ICED DESSERTS
Caramel cluster fro-yo 86
Carrot cake ice lollies 82
Frozen tiramisu slice 84
Indian-spiced Quorn ragù pot pies 55

KALE
Chicken, mushroom & kale pesto pizza 67
Fusilli with kale pesto & tomatoes 66
Kale pesto 66
Lamb shepherd's pie 34
Pesto chicken cobbler 67
Kale pesto 66
Kebab-shop houmous with
sumac chicken & onion salad 113

LAMB
Lamb shepherd's pie 34
Scotch broth 40
Lamb shepherd's pie 34
LEEKS
Pork & leek pie 26
Pesto chicken cobbler 67
LEMONS
Lemon & yogurt pancakes 90
Lemon meringue pie cake 70
Lemon & yogurt pancakes 90
Lemon meringue pie cake 70
Lentil & cauliflower dhal 46
LENTIL PASTA
Chicken & chestnut mushroom lasagne 30
Lentil spaghetti with Quorn ragù 54
LENTILS
Dhal traybake with spiced salmon 47
Lentil & cauliflower dhal 46
Roti-style wraps with dhal 47
Dhal with mango chutney chicken 46
Lentil spaghetti with Quorn ragù 54

MANGO
Crispy fish tacos with lime
slaw & mango salsa 62
Dhal with mango chutney chicken 46
Meat-feast pasta bake 109
MEATBALLS
Pork polpette 58
Pork polpette pittas with
harissa yogurt 59
Sicilian pork polpette bake 59
Sticky hoisin pork polpette with rice 58
Teriyaki mushroom meatballs
with edamame soba noodles 122
Mediterranean muffins 96
MUFFINS
Bircher muesli muffins 96
Cheese & broccoli muffins 96

Mediterranean muffins 96
Rhubarb & custard muffins 96
MUSHROOMS
Chicken & chestnut mushroom lasagne 30
Chicken, mushroom & kale pesto pizza 67
Chicken paprikash 28
Chinese soy-poached chicken
noodle soup 51
'Creamy' mushroom soup 40
Teriyaki mushroom meatballs
with edamame soba noodles 122

NOODLES
Chinese soy-poached chicken
noodle soup 51
Teriyaki mushroom meatballs
with edamame soba noodles 122
NUTS
Orange & pistachio cake 71
Pear & blueberry crumbles 76

OATS
Almond & cherry oat bars 88
Bircher muesli muffins 96
Ginger & oat biscuits 80
Teriyaki mushroom meatballs
with edamame soba noodles 122
OLIVES
Braised cod with tomatoes,
capers & olives 24
Mediterranean muffins 96
Quinoa & halloumi stuffed peppers 123
Quorn ragù tortilla bake 55
ORANGE
Orange & pistachio cake 71

PAK CHOI
Soy-poached chicken with
ginger fried rice 50
Sticky hoisin pork polpette with rice 58
PANCAKES
Chinese pancakes with
soy-poached chicken 51
Lemon & yogurt pancakes 90
PARSNIPS
Indian-spiced Quorn ragù pot pies 55
Spiced root vegetable & lentil
soup with breadsticks 124
PASTA
Chicken & chestnut mushroom lasagne 30
Braised cod with tomatoes, capers
& olives 24
Fusilli with kale pesto & tomatoes 66
Lentil spaghetti with Quorn ragù 54
Meat-feast pasta bake 109
Sicilian pork polpette bake 59
Spaghetti with chorizo crumb 107
PEARS
Pear & blueberry crumbles 76
PEAS
Chicken chipolata & prawn jambalaya 32
Fish goujons with crushed ricotta peas 63
PEPPERS
Chicken paprikash 28
Quinoa & halloumi stuffed peppers 123
Quorn ragù tortilla bake 55
PESTO
Chicken, mushroom & kale pesto pizza 67
Fusilli with kale pesto & tomatoes 66
Kale pesto 66
Pesto chicken cobbler 67

Recipe index

Goan fish curry | 20
Prawn burgers with edamame pods | 114
Seafood pies | 117
Prawn burgers with edamame pods | 114

PULSES
Beef & black bean stew | 16
Cod & butter bean fishcakes | 36
Harissa vegetable gyros | 115
Scotch broth | 40
Smoky tofu chilli pie with cornbread topping | 125
Smoky tofu chilli with quinoa | 121
White bean & saffron soup | 40

QUINOA
Crispy fish tacos with lime slaw & mango salsa | 62
Fish goujons with crushed ricotta peas | 63
Quinoa & halloumi stuffed peppers | 123
Quinoa-crusted fish goujons | 62
Smoky tofu chilli with quinoa | 121
Quinoa & halloumi stuffed peppers | 123
Quinoa-crusted fish goujons | 62

QUORN
Indian-spiced Quorn ragù pot pies | 55
Lentil spaghetti with Quorn ragù | 54
Quorn ragù tortilla bake | 55
Rich Quorn ragù | 54
Quorn ragù tortilla bake | 55

Rhubarb & custard muffins | 96
RICE
Chicken chipolata & prawn jambalaya | 32
Soy-poached chicken with ginger fried rice | 50
Sticky hoisin pork polpette with rice | 58
Rich Quorn ragù | 54
RICOTTA
Fish goujons with crushed ricotta peas | 63
Roti-style wraps with dhal | 47

SALAD
Kebab-shop houmous with sumac chicken & onion salad | 113
SALMON
Dhal traybake with spiced salmon | 47
SAUSAGES
Chicken chipolata & prawn jambalaya | 32
Seafood pies | 117
Scotch broth | 40
Sicilian pork polpette bake | 59
Slow-roasted cherry tomato pizza | 108
Smoky tofu chilli pie with cornbread topping | 125
Smoky tofu chilli with quinoa | 121
SOUP
Chinese soy-poached chicken noodle soup | 51
Chipotle butternut squash soup | 40

'Creamy' mushroom soup | 40
Scotch broth | 40
Spiced root vegetable & lentil soup with breadsticks | 124
White bean & saffron soup | 40
Soy-poached chicken breast fillets | 50
Soy-poached chicken with ginger fried rice | 50
Spaghetti with chorizo crumb | 107
Spiced root vegetable & lentil soup with breadsticks | 124
SPINACH
Cheese & broccoli muffins | 96
Chicken & chestnut mushroom lasagne | 30
Dhal with mango chutney chicken | 46
Goan fish curry | 20
Slow-roasted cherry tomato pizza | 108
Steak with cauliflower & horseradish purée | 116
Sticky hoisin pork polpette with rice | 58
Strawberry syrup cake | 71
SWEETCORN
Crispy fish tacos with lime slaw & mango salsa | 62
Fish goujons with Mexican-style rice | 63
SWEET POTATOES
Spiced root vegetable & lentil soup with breadsticks | 124
Sweet potato & goat's cheese rösti | 18

TACOS
Crispy fish tacos with lime slaw & mango salsa | 62
TARTS
Beetroot & goat's cheese tarts | 94
TOFU
Smoky tofu chilli pie with cornbread topping | 125
Smoky tofu chilli with quinoa | 121
TOMATOES
Fusilli with kale pesto & tomatoes | 66
Goan fish curry | 20
Mediterranean muffins | 96
Slow-roasted cherry tomato pizza | 108
Teriyaki mushroom meatballs with edamame soba noodles | 122

White bean & saffron soup | 40

YOGURT
Caramel cluster fro-yo | 86
Frozen tiramisu slice | 84
Greek yogurt cake | 70
Lemon & yogurt pancakes | 90
Lemon meringue pie cake | 70
Orange & pistachio cake | 71
Pork polpette pittas with harissa yogurt | 59
Strawberry syrup cake | 71

PICKLED ONIONS
Beef kofta flatbreads | 106
Fish goujons with crushed ricotta peas | 63
PIES
Indian-spiced Quorn ragù pot pies | 55
Lamb shepherd's pie | 34
Pesto chicken cobbler | 67
Pork & leek pie | 26
Seafood pies | 117
Smoky tofu chilli pie with cornbread topping | 125
PINEAPPLE
Carrot cake ice lollies | 82
PIZZA
Chicken, mushroom & kale pesto pizza | 67
Slow-roasted cherry tomato pizza | 108
PORK
Pork & leek pie | 26
Pork polpette | 58
Pork polpette pittas with harissa yogurt | 59
Sicilian pork polpette bake | 59
Sticky hoisin pork polpette with rice | 58
POTATOES
Chorizo-crusted cod with roasted cauliflower & potatoes | 105
Cod & butter bean fishcakes | 36
Indian-spiced Quorn ragù pot pies | 55
Seafood pies | 117
Steak with cauliflower & horseradish purée | 116
PRAWNS
Chicken chipolata & prawn jambalaya | 32